A Trip on the
Drunken Duchess:

Stories of World War II and Beyond

A Trip on the Drunken Duchess

Stories of World War II and Beyond

by Don Huling and Paul Huling

with additional stories by Agnes Huling and Jamie Huling

Hither Page Press

Princeton, Illinois

Dedicated to our mother, Agnes Huling,
and to all the mothers of her generation
whose sacrifices can never be fully measured.

Preface

World War II altered lives and plans on an unimaginable scale, like no event before or since. It affected lives in every city, hamlet, and community across America. Brothers, sisters, mothers, fathers, all contributed to the war effort, many in uniform, many in factories, and many at work feeding the country. Following are stories by brothers Don and Paul Huling, of La Salle, Illinois. Elder brother Don was inducted into the Army and served in the U.S. Army Air Force. He was at an air base in England on the eve of D-Day, June 6, 1944. A short time later, his squadron stormed across the English Channel to meet the Third Reich head-on. Younger brother Paul served on a Navy patrol craft at the close of the war. Their stories, both during and after the war, reflect the optimism, humor, resilience, and perseverance of the millions of Americans we came to know as "The Greatest Generation." Also included are the reflections of a mother, who, like all mothers of her time, struggled with the questions, "Will my sons be called to war? Will they return?"

CONTENTS

POST-WAR STORIES BY PAUL HULING

APPENDIX

Introduction

PRESIDENT OBAMA returned to France in 2009 to help celebrate D-Day sixty-five years after the start of the invasion to liberate Europe.

I was in southern England on June 6, 1944, when the invasion began. I was a radio operator–technician assigned to the 367th Fighter Group of the Ninth Army Air Force. There were ten of us called the CNS Gang who had all been trained in the States to operate airplane radio equipment. There existed at each airfield in England a direction-finding facility. "Dynamite" Donovan ran the 367th Fighter Group's navigational and radio equipment. Our pilots knew us as the "Dynamite" gang.

In addition to "Dynamite," our pilots could contact the 66th Fighter Wing's Control Center to use its D/F stations covering Southern England. Anyone needing a steer for home or directions to an emergency landing field could request a position fix from the 66th's D/F network. Three stations would take bearings on him and call them in to the control center for plotting. With the lost pilot's position thus pinpointed, the controller gave him his heading and distance to base. It wasn't a very sophisticated system, but it worked.

On June 4 everyone in our outfit was restricted to our airfield near Stoney Cross in Southern England. This base had been built as a glider field and had long, wide runways, the longest being 5,000 feet. We all knew the "Big Show" was about to start. We were each given a can of black or white paint and ordered to work all night on June 4–5 painting broad black and white stripes around the wings and tail booms of our P-38 planes. These stripes aided identification by other pilots and trigger-happy gunners on the ground and were applied to all Allied tactical warplanes.

Practically everyone at Stoney Cross thought the stripes had something to do with the invasion, but only a few key officers had been told about D-Day. Our Commanding Officer ordered all pilots to attend a special briefing on the evening of June 5. He told them that they would start flying patrol missions over the Channel but revealed nothing about the invasion.

The night of June 5 we listened as the air armada flew over our base headed for Normandy. In the morning we looked out at our wide runway and couldn't believe what we saw. The field was loaded with airplanes of every description that had flown that night and had been directed to land at our field. One English pilot had landed his Spitfire on the narrow blacktop highway that ended at our longest runway!

~ *Don Huling*

THE HOME FRONT

Stories by Agnes Huling

Agnes Hawthorne Huling

Pearl Harbor Day, December 7, 1941

When Dr. and Mrs. Cox called for me that Sunday afternoon, my whole thoughts were centered on the lovely Christmas program we were about to hear. The Ottawa Amateur Music Club had prepared for weeks for its annual Yuletide program, and guests were coming from miles up and down the Illinois Valley.

With the usual hustle to get ready to go, after preparing the traditional family Sunday dinner, it had not occurred to me to turn on the radio. So when my friends asked anxiously if I had heard the radio, I sensed that something unusual had happened. They had just heard the terrible news of the Japanese attack on Pearl Harbor. That was all we could speak or think about, all the way to Ottawa. It seemed so impossible and unreal!

When we came within sight of the Presbyterian Church and heard the chimes playing the old familiar carols, we lapsed once more into the Yuletide spirit. People had either not heard the awful news, or else we were trying to conceal it until after the program.

It was the most elaborate Christmas program I had ever seen, with men, women, and children taking part. The grand finale was a pageant on "Peace." What a mockery. We dreaded getting home and back into the world of Reality.

My three young sons greeted me breathlessly. It was John, the impulsive one, who spoke. "Mom, have you heard the news? We are at war! Don shall go first, then I, and then Paul."

What would a mother reply?

Reactions

Don's reaction was, "I want to stay in school as long as I can, then when my turn comes, I will go and make the best soldier that I know how." So he finished his first year in engineering at junior college, took a special government course in the Missouri School of Mines at Rolla in the summer of 1942, then entered his sophomore year at J.C. By the beginning of 1943, we all realized his civilian days were numbered.

In the meantime, the draft age had been lowered to 18 and soon Johnny would get his turn, so we thought. That would leave only Paul. He was absorbed in his high school activities, with work at the Travis Garage after school and on Saturdays.

It was at this stage in our lives that a desperate idea seized me. Pleas were coming in over the air waves, in newspapers, from lecture platforms, and finally through handbills strewn at the doorsteps: "All women who have no small children and are physically fit MUST volunteer for war work—or be conscripted like the men who do the fighting." After all, was there any good reason why I couldn't or shouldn't volunteer for a war job?

Green River Ordnance Plant

So one bleak morning in February, 1943, I boarded a bus for the GROP near Dixon, Illinois. It was a ride of 45 minutes, but if others could take it, so could I!

The personnel building was packed, and all applicants who could physically qualify were accepted and given whatever job was most fitting and urgent. When my turn came, I was informed that a ladies' dormitory was soon to be opened. House mothers were needed. I had the qualifications. Would I be willing to come back in a week and officially open the dorm? I would. Of course, there was some red tape. From

ABOVE: **Women on an ordnance line; RIGHT: Worker numbers**

a preliminary interview in La Salle, my references had been followed up. There were interviews by heads of Personnel and Industrial Relations and finally William Steinwedell himself, who is General Manager. He explained to me the purpose of the dorm, which was to house those who should soon be sent in from long distances. The house mothers were to do their best in making these weary, homesick women comfortable.

Thanksgiving Day, 1943

If I shall live to be 100, I can't forget that Thanksgiving Day of 1943.

The Allies were going strong on all fronts. The Italian

invasion was well underway and our men in the Pacific were at long last "slapping the Japs."

Munitions from GROP were much in demand. All fall, many lines had worked on Sundays. Foremen and key personnel had worked double shifts. Everyone had worked under pressure.

Day and night the huge munitions trucks were being loaded from the lines, thence to the railroad shipping terminals, where they were sent to their destinations. All addresses being in code, no one knew exactly where the boxes would eventually land.

In the midst of this feverish activity, bulletins were posted in change houses throughout the area, to the effect that every worker must report for work on Thanksgiving Day, the same as usual.

Small groups gathered around the bulletin. Soon it became a large group. Which way would the psychology jump?

First, a few groans of disgust and disappointment. Then a few who had no home ties ventured the remark that maybe it wouldn't be so bad. "After all, girls, if we're needed so, we can't let down our boys."

Then the matron spoke. "Girls, most of us have worked hard every Thanksgiving since we can remember. If getting up a big family dinner isn't work, what is? Let's make the usual feast a simple meal and come out here gladly to do our part."

The tide had turned and every woman had eyes which glowed with pride as she thought how her company, her country and boys needed Her.

Soon plans were underway for a potluck dinner to which the entire line would be included. The squad leaders assumed responsibility for the planning. Women who lived on farms or in villages were asked to bring fried chickens. Others were asked to prepare various kinds of salads, vegetables, cakes, and pumpkin pies. The array of home-cooked foods was a welcome sight to the cafeteria-hardened war workers.

For once all bays quit at the same time, and by noon all were assembled around the tables in the bomb shelter. There was a hushed expectancy—then the firm voice of our superintendent, big, brawny "Red" Ed Ahlenius, who asked us to bow in prayer. We had all had great admiration for Ed as a leader of industry. Now, we had great respect for him as a Christian gentleman, for the prayer he offered was timely and sincere. When he asked God's blessing on all of our soldier boys, both in camps at home and at the fronts, there were no dry eyes in the place. Some of the young war wives could hardly refrain from weeping audibly, but nevertheless, it was one of those occasions when no one felt abashed to show feelings.

It was a sober but grateful crowd which sat down to partake of the food. Line 6 was just one big happy family on that Thanksgiving Day.

Presently, two musicians appeared. Each had an accordion. They gave us some jolly duos, then suggested that we request songs that all could sing. "Pistol Packin' Mama" was by far the most popular number. The poor boys could hardly find a place to quit.

At one P.M. when a slight lull took place, someone requested our National Anthem. With one accord, we all rose and sang our anthem as we had never sung before. Silence. A whistle blew. Each man and woman back to his post.

Was our production record up to expectations that day? Our bosses answered, "Yes!"

D-Day, June 6, 1944

This is "D-day" for which we have been waiting so long!

About the time I was dropping into bed at 2:15 A.M. our boys were landing on the Normandy beaches. Had I known, there would have been no sleep for me, but as it was, I was awakened about 8 A.M. by the blare of the radio. Neighbors were out in their yards, talking tensely. I could sense the news, even before I was told!

Hastening downstairs in bathrobe and slippers, I listened to the dramatic recital of the accomplishments of "our boys" and the prediction that they were headed for "one of the toughest fights in history."

A lump came into my throat and I struggled resolutely to hold back the tears. Where was our soldier boy Don today? The last we had heard he was somewhere in England, preparing for the invasion. Yesterday a letter came to Simmon the Florist from Dundee, Angus. It was dated May 13 and contained an order for flowers to be delivered to Mrs. Donald Huling on June 2 (wedding anniversary).

As the announcers spoke with enthusiasm of our huge air armada and our superiority in the skies, my thoughts were also with the boys behind the lines who were there to keep 'em flying. Yes, we are sure that somewhere in that awful maelstrom called Hitler's Fortress Europe, our Don is there with thousands of other fine lads, doing his bit for home and country.

What did I do today? I had planned to continue painting the hall—and that is just what I did! After all, I had more urges to paint and fix up home than I did even yesterday. For wouldn't the war be over sooner now? Everyone predicts that this is the beginning of the end. "When the boys come home" is the slogan on everyone's lips today.

When arriving for duty at GROP I was told that everyone

had been in a state of excitement all day there. We mothers who have sons in service felt an even closer tie than we had.

When the tired and dirty workers came up from the lines tonight I greeted them with—"Girls, the radio announcers are telling what a fine job your grenades are doing today!" They were serious and silent. Tears gleamed in the eyes of several.

Another group has gone out tonight to make more instruments of destruction. The change house is quiet. I look at Don's picture, then at the invasion map. Where is he? The good times we all had together on his last furlough come to mind. Over and above it all, his cheery words of comfort to me— "Everything will turn out for the best, Mom. Don't worry!"

Thanksgiving 1944

The incoming shift announced that the first snow of the season was falling.

As we assembled in the bomb shelter bundled up for our long ride home, word was passed around in whispers that Dave had just had word that his brother John was missing in action over Germany. It was a quiet, subdued shift which clocked out that Thanksgiving morning at 12:30 A.M.

Dave was a favorite of all. He was our boss on the Red Shift and was himself quite a hero, having been injured in a football game in his youth and spending eight years as an invalid. Although he had a twisted back, otherwise he was a handsome man and a jolly good fellow. His mother—"Ma" to all of us—had raised a large family, including several sons. Now, with too much time to think, she had come to work at the plant. Along with her came her youngest daughter and two in-laws. One of these was the very attractive blond wife of her heroic son, John, the bombardier.

Everyone loved Doris, too. No task was too hard. She came in with blistered hands many times—but always with a smile and quiet dignity. So our hearts went out to this dear and saddened family.

The snow fell just enough to make things lovely. The trip home seemed short. In the kitchen at 2 A.M. sat Paul and Daddy. The former had been to a Union Thanksgiving service at the church, thence to a party. Dad had been down to the plant with Mattie (Mr. Mathis of Easton) seeing how the tests were turning out relative to the making of special Hi-cement. We enjoyed a snack together, thence to bed until 9 A.M.

Things had to click and they did. The cornucopia graced the table as usual, with its content of fruit. But it was a different group which gathered round the table. Don and John were missing, but Christie sat with us in her highchair and nibbled on bits of this and that. She had her first lollypop for dessert.

After a blessing by Paul we had the following: baked chicken, a pheasant, escalloped potatoes, baked Hubbard squash, relishes, lettuce salad, and pumpkin pie with whipped cream. Alice provided salad and dessert.

After a brief dinner visit, here was the car for Green River! George presented each of his riders with a piece of possum which he had prepared himself (um).

The shift assembled in 418 as usual. Dave was there and so was Doris, her eyes starry with tears and cheeks pale, but the same sweet smile for all of us. When later she came up for her coat and we were alone, she said, "Did you know that John is missing in action?" I replied, "Yes, I have thought of you all constantly and hope that he shall return to you unharmed as so many of the boys have." She said that at first she could not cry, but eventually she did, then made up her mind to be brave and carry on, always hoping for the best.

"Ma" at first had gone all to pieces, cried, screamed, and

been altogether hysterical. Then a calm descended on her. She would have been at her job, as usual, too, if her family would have permitted. But as she had a bad heart for some time, they would not permit it. The cafeteria was a busy place, as a turkey dinner had been prepared for the workers. The matrons assisted in serving.

Dave had taken some of the employees over to visit Line 1, where they were turning out the big shells. Doris went, too. When she returned, she said, "I saw a girl whose husband was killed in action. She doesn't even have hope. But I do." With that she lifted her chin a bit higher and left me alone to ponder.

Lieutenant John did not return. After a few more weeks of waiting, his family was honored by receiving his posthumous awards from our government.

Pearl Harbor Day, December 7, 1944

Although our historians shall record December 7, 1941, as the date of the Japanese attack, to me, the second Sunday in December shall always be the day of memories.

Three years ago, we were shocked into the awful reality that our country was forced into a war for which we were unprepared! Three years ago tonight, our united family hovered around the radio while details of the massacre of "our boys" filtered through. Underneath it all was the realization that our days of being together were numbered. As a mother with three young sons, I could not fail to read the handwriting on the wall.

Today was a day of appraisal. As I hung clean curtains for the Christmas holiday, I touched against our small satin service flag. Visions of Don came to me—as he looked when he came home with the flag and proudly hung it himself in the window. Immediately after he had passed his physical, he had been inducted.

He had come home from school one day, whistling as usual. On the shelf under the long mirror was a long brown envelope with "War Department" in the upper left hand corner. He spied it at once, ripped it open, waved it at me, and said, "Uncle Sam needs me!" Now he is somewhere in France, having crossed the Channel not long after D-Day.

Service Flag: red with blue star

PART I

War Era Stories by Don Huling

Corporal Don Huling

The Start of the "Big Adventure"

I was inducted into the Army on my nineteenth birthday, February 15, 1943. I led the largest contingent of young men drafted from the La Salle-Peru-Oglesby area up to this point of the war. The article and picture in the *Post-Tribune*, La Salle, Illinois, reads as follows—"Comprising the largest single contingent of 100 selectees to leave the Tri-Cities in one day, these young men submitted to physical examinations at a medical station in Peoria. The group was under the leadership of Don Huling. Those in today's contingent will have the privilege of joining the Navy, Marine Corps, Coast Guard or Army."

Those of us who passed the physical in Peoria and were assigned to the Army were bussed to Scott Field near Rantoul, Illinois. We were issued army clothing, which made us laugh the first time we put on our fatigues. I can still see Teddy Yelich sticking toilet paper on a cut on his face he made with his newly issued GI razor blade. We were given a battery of written tests, and as a result I ended up in the Army Air Corp headed for Chicago and Radio School after three months of Basic Training at Sheppard Field, Texas.

Basic Training, for me, was great sport. It fit right in with my scouting experiences. As Boy Scouts, we had lined up at attention, practiced marching and hiking and found night activities such as capture the flag challenging. So when we had to do all of these as part of Basic Training, I was ready.

I shipped out of Texas by train and landed in Chicago. We were billeted in the Congress Hotel, right near Lake Shore Drive. I failed the Morse Code class. That, plus my poor eyesight, meant I couldn't become a radio operator on any of the B-17 or B-24 bombers. Those that passed got to fly, man the radios, and fire machine guns. I'm glad I flunked out. Instead I was assigned to continue school in Madison, Wisconsin, and Tomah, Wisconsin, where we eventually became radio technicians proficient in the Control Network System (CNS).

Our Wedding, June 2, 1943

Our wedding picture was taken in front of Peru Hospital and is the only picture we have of our wedding. My sister Alice was in the hospital with her first child, Christie, who had just been born. Lindy and I visited them before we left by train for Chicago and our very short honeymoon. But let me backtrack for a little bit.

I called Lindy from Sheppard Field, Texas, where we were sent for two months of basic training before getting sent to Chicago early in May to study radio. I asked her to marry me if I could get a weekend pass once I got up north. She said "yes" quite casually, which puzzled me as I thought she would be thrilled. Her dad was standing right next to her, it turned out, and she wasn't sure how she was going to break the news to her folks and mine.

I told the fellows on my floor of the Congress Hotel that I was going to get married down in La Salle the very first weekend I could get a pass. June 2 was the first weekend we had off and we all passed inspection. I ran down to the La Salle Street Railroad Station in Chicago, grabbed the first train available, and landed in La Salle Sunday night. Monday my dad, Thurman, drove Lindy and me to Ottawa to get our marriage license. That afternoon was the big day.

My brother John was the best man. Onalee, Lindy's sister, was Matron of Honor. My dad had given me written permission to marry Lindy. The wedding took place about 4:00 P.M. in the Congregational Church. We figured it would be a small wedding in the middle of the week, as most of our young friends were in school or in the service. It turned out the church was full of our families' friends and a few relatives. Rev. George McClary performed the ceremony in fifteen minutes. I got flustered when I tried to say, "With this ring." It came out, "With this wing I thee wed." Onalee started to giggle. When it came time to kiss the bride, though, I rose to the occasion. Lindy had asked me not to just give her a little peck on the cheek. I grabbed her, bent her over, and gave her a real kiss! She struggled a little as I was having fun and wouldn't let her go. I still remember taking her hand and almost running down the aisle to the front of the church.

My mother, Agnes, had prepared supper for us before we left by train for Chicago. We first visited Alice in the Peru Hospital. Supper was baked beans and all the trimmings which was not very romantic for two kids getting ready to depart on their honeymoon!

Lindy and I had both done some preliminary work prior to the week of June 2. Lindy had come to Chicago with her mother, who was president of the La Salle Women's Club and was attending the annual convention in Chicago. Lindy was able to land a job at the Chicago Title and Trust Company that started two days after we were married. I was able to find an apartment up on Lawrence Avenue. We finally found the apartment about 2 A.M. on our wedding night.

Our send-off from La Salle was memorable. We had a couple of suitcases full of clothing and pots and pans ready to set up housekeeping. As the train was pulling out of the station, Larry, Onalee's husband, waved my pajama bottoms at me. He had removed them from our suitcase! Oh well, who needs pajama bottoms on their wedding night anyway?

I reported back to the Congress Hotel the day after our

wedding. Lindy reported for work the next day. One week later I was in Madison, Wisconsin. The army had other plans for me. No setting up housekeeping yet!

AWOL?

Lindy and I didn't see much of each other after our wedding, as I had to stay at the Congress Hotel that first week. In fact our honeymoon consisted of one night in our apartment up on Lawrence Avenue. One week after we were married I was transferred to Madison, Wisconsin, for advanced radio school.

I found a room in Madison. A couple weeks later Lindy arrived from La Salle, where she had been recuperating after our one night together in Chicago. She had a job with the Chicago Title and Trust company, where she worked for a week after I left. But we both wanted to be together as much as possible before I finished my training. I knew I could be shipped to the Pacific or the European Theater of Operations, as by now I had a pretty good idea of what we were being trained to do.

The room in Madison was near campus and was terrible. In fact, it was so bad the lady that lived in the house next door helped Lindy find a much nicer room the very next day. We still hadn't gotten together after about three weeks of marriage. I was getting desperate, but it looked like I was stuck out at Truax Field until I could get a pass.

Friday night finally arrived and I was the first GI in line to get my weekend pass. Our Sergeant would hand out our pass when we stepped up and gave our name and Serial Number. My number was 36475099. We were instructed to go to the next table, sign our name and serial number and under the columns OUT and IN mark down the time we left base and returned. Maybe I was excited about seeing Lindy or just thinking ahead, but once I got my pass, I walked right by the next table and out the door, where I caught the bus that was waiting to take a bunch of us into Madison.

Sunday night when I returned I realized I could hang onto my pass just by keeping my mouth shut. That way I could visit Lindy every day, except there was one serious problem. Our Advanced Radio School was on three shifts and took place in buildings on the field. When we weren't in school for eight hours we were to fall out for PE (Physical Education), eat our meals on base, and kill some time before turning in for lights-out at 9:00 P.M.

We were on three shifts, and within each ninety-man barracks, men were coming and going at around 11 P.M. The sergeant in charge of the barracks would check our name tags, which we were instructed to keep at the foot of our bunks, and list our Radio School Class Number. If an empty bunk belonged to a GI who was supposed to be in school, Sarge was satisfied everything was fine. Since they also took roll at the beginning of each school shift, it looked like they had a foolproof system. Until I showed up, that is.

I confided to my buddies who I had been with in Chicago. They knew I had just gotten married, and that I planned to go into town every day to be with my newlywed wife, but that I'd never miss a day of school. I'd never be AWOL from school.

The solution was pretty simple. Since Sarge only did the bed check after 9:00 P.M. all I had to do was indicate on my bed tag the number of the class that was in school on the afternoon shift that day. It worked like a charm. I'd go to school every day and spend the rest of the summer day with my sweetheart.

I did have one close call, however. The phone rang at 4:00 A.M. one morning from one of my buddies. He was desperate. The captain in charge of the base was pulling a surprise bed check at 7:00 A.M. and I had no excuse for not being there. "Don," he said, "You better get your butt out here on the double!" Wouldn't you know it—the busses didn't start running until 7:00 A.M. There was nothing I could do but face the music once I got back to camp.

Well, it turned out I wasn't the only GI out to beat the system. When I didn't turn up on time, my buddies folded up my cot and hid it in the rafters above the latrine. Captain and Sarge never missed me.

AWOL? I never missed a day of school. I saved the army the food I would have eaten if I'd stayed out at camp. However, in retrospect, and as the fires of youth start to subside, I realize the system would not have worked as well as it did if everyone who wanted to be with their loved ones had pulled the stunt I was guilty of that beautiful summer of 1943.

A Marine for a Week

Lindy accompanied me to all of my U.S. posts after our marriage on June 2, 1943. We started out at 185 Lawrence Avenue, Chicago, in a one-room apartment. I had found it advertised in the *Chicago Tribune* and rented it a couple weeks before our marriage. I was transferred to Truax Field near Madison, Wisconsin. Lindy followed me north in a couple weeks after she closed up the rented apartment, quit her job at the Chicago Title and Trust Company, and lugged our pots and pans to the post office for shipment to La Salle. After a second try in Madison, Lindy found a bedroom near downtown which worked out pretty well for us that summer.

Lindy found a job at Renanbaums Drug Store just across the street from the University of Wisconsin. One day a lady from a bakery up the street asked Lindy if she would like to work for her. Lindy impressed her with how nicely she handled the rather aloof university students who hung out at the soda fountain. Lindy took the job and stuck with it until I was sent to advanced radio school in Tomah, Wisconsin. Lindy returned home for the second time while I was getting settled up north.

Lindy arrived after about a month, but Tomah was so small and my stay so short all we were able to do was find a room. It was an upstairs room with an older couple. It was heated from below through an open vent in the floor. We got out to the Army camp a couple of times, but all in all it wasn't as nice as Madison. To make it a little more exciting, I became a Marine for a week in order to be with Lindy every possible moment I could.

We had inspection of our barracks every Saturday morning. My bunk was always made, since I hadn't slept in it since Lindy arrived. One Saturday the inspector arrived with a fly swatter in hand. In order to pass the inspection, his fly swatter had to sort of bounce back when he swatted the blanket. Well, wouldn't you know it, when he swatted my blanket there was a cloud of dust.

"Take this man's pass," he shouted. "He doesn't get off base for week."

A small contingent of Marines was going to school at the same time we were finishing our training in the CNS. I had introduced Lindy to these guys during one of our early visits to the camp. When I confided my predicament to one of these Marines, he offered to loan me his pass so I could leave camp. This sounded sort of risky to me, but I had noticed the guards were rather lax. All we had to do to get off base was smile, act nice and respectful, and flash our pass, which they didn't even look at.

"I'll give it a try," I said. The rewards of being with Lindy far outweighed anything they might do to me if I got caught. And that's how I became a Marine for a week!

Off to Europe

Everyone who finished CNS training was assigned to an Army Air Force squadron. In my case, it was the 367th Fighter Group, 392nd Fighter Squadron, stationed in California. Lindy had returned home for the third time while I finished training and spent a week in the hospital recuperating from a viral infection. My stay in the hospital put me a week behind and kept me from graduating with the class that wound up going to the Pacific Theater of Operations. As it was, I was the last man to join the CNS Gang in California.

I got a two-week furlough with orders to report to Fresno, California, the first week in January, 1944. Lindy and I enjoyed a few days at home.

We boarded the Rock Island Rocket for Chicago a couple days after Christmas with a duffel bag and one suitcase. My orders were to join the 367th Fighter Group in Fresno. The train was packed with soldiers and sailors and a few women. The cars were antique with hard benches for seats. We toughed it out for three days and nights, sitting up all the way. When we got to Fresno, Lindy found out that jobs were scarce. She finally found one in a laundry where she wound up sorting dirty bed sheets. I reported for duty with the 392nd Fighter Squadron, which had moved out to Sacramento on December 10. Lindy and I shipped out and caught up with the squadron in Sacramento.

We found a room on the third floor of a boarding house, and I was able to get a pass every day to get into town. Lindy didn't get a job in Sacramento as she wasn't feeling very well.

I came in from "work" one evening and discovered she had a fever. She had passed out on the steps up to our apartment. A woman who lived on the third floor next to us had just stepped over her rather than lend a helping hand. Turned out she was the wife of one of our officers at the base. This kind of snobbery was more common among the officers' wives and enlisted men's wives than either of us realized. Anyway, I found a thermometer which I washed off before using and took her temperature. 108 degrees! Something was really wrong. Then I remembered I had washed off the thermometer in hot water and had never shaken it down.

One day we went walking in Governor's Park. I saw an olive tree with what looked like ripe olives to me. I picked one and gave it to Lindy to taste. It was terrible. She accused me of pulling this stunt on purpose, but I really didn't know that the olives had to be processed before they were good to eat.

Our pilots had been training with the 367th since its activation at Hamilton Field, California, in mid-July, 1943. The group's assignment was operational training on the P-39 fighter aircraft. The final phase of training, including gunnery, bombing, and simulated tactical missions, began when the group moved to northern California. I realized our time in the States was getting short, so Lindy and I decided she would return to La Salle rather than stay in California, where her only relative was her mother's brother Bruce.

Lindy visited Uncle Bruce and Aunt Hilma before heading home to La Salle. Glenn had sent her $75.00 for the train ticket and Bruce had given her $5.00 to help with any other expenses. I met her as she was boarding the train in San Jose. She didn't know I was making a last desperate effort to see her before we parted—for how long, we didn't know. Her hair was up in pin curls. She was really surprised to see me. The train was loaded with sailors returning from the Pacific. Some were old enough to be her father. I got off the train in Sacramento and never felt as low as I did at that moment. Lindy kept a stiff upper lip and waved to me as the train left the station. I gulped, wiped the tears from my eyes, and headed back to camp and the great adventure that lay ahead.

We did have one more chance to say good-bye before I shipped out to the European Theater of Operations. The 367th Fighter Group boarded a troop train in Sacramento and headed across the country bound for Camp Shanks, New York. As the train slowly worked its way through Chicago, I was able to jump off and make a phone call to Lindy. She was at home with her folks. It was about two in the morning when Glenn, her father, answered the phone. "Lindy," he said, "it's for you." I told her we were heading for the ETO and not the Pacific and that I'd call every night as long as I could. The night she did not receive the call, she knew I was on my way.

A Trip on the Drunken Duchess

August 2, 2002

I was watching public TV a week ago and a new book entitled *Tuxedo Park* was reviewed. It is the story of Alfred Lee Loomis, a Wall Street tycoon of the 1920s and '30s who amassed a huge fortune, then used it and all his energy to help win WWII.

The book's jacket copy reads as follows: "In the fall of 1940, as German bombers flew over London and with America not yet at war, a small team of British scientists, on orders from Winston Churchill, carried out a daring transatlantic mission, which was to carry British military secrets to America."

I was amazed to read that Edward "Taffy" Bowen, a British scientist who was carrying Britain's most valuable

The Drunken Duchess

military secrets, including the latest radar developments, recalled that the name of the ship they boarded for America was the Duchess of Bedford. The Duchess earned her nickname "Drunken Duchess" for the way she would "roll all over the high seas."

Our outfit boarded this same ship the end of March 1944. Accommodations on the ship for officers included staterooms for captains and higher ranks and triple-deck bunks for lieutenants, while the enlisted men were packed into the lower decks. Captain Jack Reed observed that there would be "one beautiful mess when this tub hits open sea." And he was right on! Those fortunate enough to find space slung hammocks while the rest scrounged sleeping space on tables or on the decks.

I was one of the lucky ones and found a hammock right away. Once out to sea, where we joined a large convoy all headed for Europe, the old Canadian passenger ship started to roll and almost everyone got sea sick. I was able to get out of my "bed" and head for the railing. I learned that walking on the deck in the fresh air helped to keep the food down, so that is what two or three of us fellows from the CNS Gang did. The food was so terrible, we lived on peanuts we were able to buy from the ship's store.

We landed in Glasgow, Scotland, April 3, 1944. After an all night ride that took us through blacked-out London, we arrived at our airfield in southern England, known as Stoney Cross. The pilots had hoped to find P-51s waiting for them at this field, but instead found nothing but P-38s. Already low from weeks of travel, their spirits sank a little more as they gazed on this depressing collection of twin-engine monsters.

"Well, that's just about the last straw," quipped Captain Jimmy Peck, the RAF veteran and hero of Malta. As he uttered the phrase, he had only one more week to live.

The V-1 Flying Bomb

February 13, 2002

I find I have time on my hands during these chemo sessions so I am catching up with some serious reading. I have re-read Doris Kearns Goodwin's *No Ordinary Time: Franklin and Eleanor Roosevelt: The Home Front in World War II* and I'm almost finished reading Merle Miller's *Ike the Soldier as They Knew Him*. Both books have mentioned subjects and times I recall living through. On page 520 of Goodwin's book she talks about the V-1 flying bomb the Germans started shooting at London early in 1944.

Al Keim and I were in London on a weekend pass while those bombs were coming in. They were rocket-powered craft launched from giant concrete bunkers in German-occupied territory in northen France. The V-1 carried more than 12,000 pounds of high explosives and fell indiscriminately on people and buildings alike. In two weeks, nearly 3000 people had been killed and over 10,000 wounded.

Al and I didn't know these statistics or we might have acted differently. We got a room on the third floor of a cheap hotel near the heart of London. We were just climbing into our beds when we heard a V-1 chugging in. We had been told that the bomb was ready to drop when the engines stopped. We weren't about to hang

Al Keim

around when this first one came in. We threw on our shirts and trousers and ran down all three flights of stairs. It kept chugging as it passed overhead and eventually went off with a loud bang. We climbed back up all three flights of stairs and tried to get some sleep when a second one came in. So it was run down three flights, wait, and climb back up three flights. When the third one came in we said the heck with it. We became fatalists. If our number was up, it didn't matter if we were upstairs or downstairs.

Salisbury Cathedral

If sin is turning away from God, here are two stories that illustrate this point.

The first story is about a man who is driving his car down a superhighway on his way home when he gets this strong urge to get off the straight path and try one he knows he shouldn't. He gets off at the next interchange and doesn't know whether to turn right or left. He turns left and is too proud to ask how to get home. He finally stops and asks directions. He is told kindly to turn around and go back. When he gets home, he asks his wife for forgiveness for being late and going astray. She forgives him and in essence says, "Go and sin no more."

The second story is a true story I shared today with the men in my Men's Bible Study. I had planned to write this story for my grandchildren as a cute World War II experience. I now realize there is a lot more to this story than an experience with a funny ending.

I was in southern England during WWII prior to the Normandy invasion. Our pilots were learning to fly the Lockheed P-38s they found parked at our field near Southampton. That gave me and two of my buddies time to go exploring. We decided to visit Salisbury Cathedral. We joined a group of about thirty other GIs with a guide who told us the history of this fine church and explained the layout and why the nave always pointed east toward Jerusalem.

When we got to the high altar, my curious buddies and I noticed what looked like a door to one side that the guide failed to talk about. "What could be behind that door?" we asked each other. "Let's find out." We hung behind the tour group and guide, and when they had left, we tried the door, opened it, and stepped behind the altar into a little room. Off to one side was another room that we figured was a confessional. There was a table with a beautiful hand-crafted doily that caught my eye. On the shelves were three or four bottles of wine we figured were to be used for communion. Well, temptation got the upper hand, and we wound up emptying all three bottles. The doily became even more attractive, and I grabbed it and put it in my pocket.

When we emerged from behind the altar, the guide was quite upset. He thought he had lost us. We weren't lost—just misguided.

I carried that doily with me through France and Germany for the rest of the war. I brought it home and tried to display it on an end table we had near an east window. Something was wrong! I had told my wife how I had "liberated" it, but she and I felt it should not be displayed. We were both too proud to tell our friends the truth.

About five years ago my wife and I took a trip to England and I had a chance to return the doily. We had visited Salisbury Cathedral and I had not found the correct or comfortable opportunity to return it and confess my sin to someone. Outside in the fresh air and sunshine I took a deep breath and resolved to try once more. I returned inside and found an usher for a wedding that was taking place that afternoon. I told him my story, gave him the doily, and hastily retreated from the church.

When we returned to the States, I decided to write a letter to the head of the church and ask him for forgiveness. I received a letter back from him in which he stated he could not forgive me—that was between me and God—but for $100 I could become a lifetime member of the Friends of Salisbury Cathedral.

I mailed him a check the next day.

What does the Bible say about sin?

Galatians 6:1-2 "Brothers, if someone is caught in a sin, you who are spiritual should restore him gently. But watch yourself, or you also may be tempted. Carry each other's burdens, and in this way you will fulfill the law of Christ."

1 John 1:9 "If we confess our sins, He is faithful and just and will forgive us our sins and purify us from all unrighteousness."

THE FRIENDS OF SALISBURY CATHEDRAL

Hon. Secretary: P.A. SUMMERFIELD

Patron: THE LORD BISHOP OF SALISBURY
President: THE LORD LIEUTENANT OF WILTSHIRE
Chairman of the Council: THE DEAN OF SALISBURY

52, THE CLOSE,
SALISBURY,
WILTSHIRE,
SP1 2EL

SALISBURY (0722) 335161

Mr Donald J Huling   4th December 1991
P O Box 1155
La Salle
Il 91301
USA

Dear Mr. Huling,

Thank you for your letter of 25th November. The item you returned is
what is known as a "Corporal", i.e. a cloth on which to place conse-
crated elements. The Head Verger, who remembers its return, tells me
that it is now kept in the Vestry with the stock of similar items.

The fact that the cloth was in your possession for something like 45
years is obviously still troubling you, although you have made the
effort to return it. It is not really my place to forgive you as you
ask, for the cloth was not my property nor that of the Friends of the
Cathdral. However, I am sure that we all understand the impulses of
youth and full allowance can be made for your indiscretion. I think
you can rest assured that the Cathedral authorities are grateful for
the return of the artefact and hold nothing against you.

I wonder if you would like to become a "Friend of the Cathedral" and
enclose a leaflet which gives details of our work and incorporates an
application form.

With all good wishes,
Yours sincerely,

P.A. Summerfield
Secretary.

12/7/91   FOR $200.00

ENCLOSED IS MY CHECK # 1099 AND APPLICATION FORM
FOR LIFE MEMBERSHIP OF THE FRIENDS OF SALISBURY
CATHEDRAL.
I NOW HAVE ANOTHER REASON TO RETURN TO ENGLAND —
TO MEET YOU AND REVIST THE CATEDRAL.

Donald J. Huling

Registered Charity No. 243439

Romans 6:13 "Do not let sin reign in your mortal body so that you obey its evil desires. . . . Rather offer yourselves to God, as those who have been brought from death to life."

Romans 8:1 "Therefore, there is now no condemnation for those who are in Christ Jesus, because through Christ Jesus the law of the Spirit of life set me free from the law of sin and death."

Major Joe Griffin

On page 35 of the book *The Dynamite Gang* by Richard Groh is a picture of Capt. Joe Griffin and his brother Tech. Sgt. James Griffin. The members of the CNS Gang that were present in Pittsburgh for the 40th Reunion of the 367th Fighter Group had the pleasure of meeting Joe and discussing in detail some of the air battles that led to our group receiving the Army Presidential Unit Citation.

The CNS Gang was stationed away from the rest of the members of the fighter group where we manned the radio equipment. As a result we never really got to know any of the pilots we were supporting when they were flying missions. The Gang was recognized at the reunion weekend, and during the talk we had with Major Joe he made us feel we had made a real contribution to the war effort.

One of the stories Joe told was the raid the 367th made near Cherbourg, France, on June 22, 1944. He returned from this mission with 405 holes in his P-38 plane. Major Robert E. Smith, whom Joe had flown with as a member of the Flying Tigers in the China-Burma-India Theater, was killed in this battle. I could tell Joe still missed his buddy.

Another story Joe told us was the time Tony Levier, who was a test pilot for Lockheed, put on a show at our southern England airfield to convince our pilots what a really good

The Dynamite Gang (376th Fighter Group). FRONT: Don Huling, Pat Tramontozzi, Warren Wakefield, Andy Cummins; BACK: Toxie Griffith, E.E. (Edge) Caudle, Dan Morse, Al Keim, Ray Abeta, George Roman.

plane the P-38 was to fly. This demonstration came shortly after we had lost Jimmy Peck in an accident as he was trying to land the "bird" for the first time. After putting on a great aerial show, Tony wound it up by diving straight down to gain speed, pulling back on the stick and going into a loop with both motors stopped and props feathered, then landing and rolling up to the pilots who were watching in amazement, and dipping the nose by applying the brakes to the front wheel. I remember watching this show from a distance and thinking "what a plane!"

Joe told us about shooting down two German FW 190s on August 13, 1944. The story follows.

The 392nd took off for Chartres and another armed reconnaissance. Finding plenty of targets, Major Joe Griffin's flight dropped its bombs and climbed to act as top cover, while the other pilots made their bombing runs. Swiveling their heads in search of enemy planes, the four top cover men orbited the area at 8000 feet.

Griffin saw them first. Only gray specks against the green patchwork below, but within seconds he identified fourteen FW 190s climbing toward him. He radioed the sighting to the rest of the squadron and took his flight down to bounce them.

A savage dogfight ensued with additional enemy aircraft joining in. When it ended, smoke from ten destroyed German fighters curled up from the ground, and the 392nd claimed five more damaged.

The battle that affected us the most took place on August 25, 1944. The 367th returned to enemy airfields near Laon, France, and got a hot reception. Joining the 394th squadron, Major Griffin brought the 392nd into the fight from out of the sun. He shot down one German and damaged another. In a superb exhibition of flying and marksmanship, Captain Larry Blumer shot down five enemy aircraft and became an "Ace" in one day. The 367th Fighter Group received the Presidential Unit Citation, the highest possible award for a unit in combat.

Paris, France

The first time we got to Paris was in the fall of 1944. Three other CNS Gang members and I drove off the Red Ball Highway right into town and parked our radio truck almost under the Eiffel Tower. We were greeted as liberators, as

DeGaul had entered the city in front of his troops only a couple of months earlier. The people we met that day were hungry for American cigarettes, candy bars and soap, and we were prepared to furnish them some of these luxuries they had been deprived of while under the German authority. We didn't have a lot to share, but when we opened the side doors of the truck and indicated we had goodies to sell, we were mobbed.

But let me back up a little. I thought we were in Europe to fight a war—not go sightseeing. So here is how Al Keim, Pat Tramontozzi, George Roman and I ended up near the Eiffel Tower that September day back in 1944.

The 392nd Fighter Squadron had moved to field A10 near Carentan on July 27, then to A2 near Isigny on August 14. This field was near enough to Utah Beach that some of the fellows walked down to the sea looking for souvenirs. All three of the squadrons in the 367th Fighter Group were together at this field until we split up and moved on September 12. We were headed for St. Quentin, which is north and east of Paris. The 392nd was the last squadron to leave A2. The other two squadrons went ahead and set up the equipment at the new field. We were in no rush to get around Paris as the other CNS men were up ahead operating the radio equipment.

By September, General George Patton and his Third Army had broken out of St. Lo and had the enemy almost surrounded in the Falaise Gap. Our pilots were flying every day, helping the ground troops whenever called upon. Patton had the German forces on the run and claimed he would have gotten all the way to Berlin if he hadn't run out of gasoline and winter supplies.

Anyway, Patton sent our fighter group loot he had "liberated" in his mad dash across France. Our supply officer

Don, Pat, and Al
September 1944
Paris

FROM LEFT: Wake, Pat, Andy, Toxie

picked up cigars and wine that he brought back and rationed out to us boys—compliments of George!

I never knew how my buddy Pat got all those cigars until he told this story much later. We all had ration cards we received the day we left England for France. Once a month we would pick up goodies: a couple of candy bars, a bar of soap, and a carton of cigarettes. When they started passing out cigars, Pat traded his cigarette ration for the cigars that had been given to us by General Patton. Since I didn't smoke, I accumulated cigarettes rapidly. When we got to Paris, I was loaded.

That day I sold everything that I had accumulated. I probably could have sold the entire lot to one person who would have turned around and made a big profit. Instead, I sold one pack at a time to the crowd who kept pressing closer. I was accumulating French francs that looked like "funny money" to me. My steel helmet was full of the stuff when I got through. I later sent Lindy a check for $300 that made her wonder what I was doing over there.

One of the people in the crowd was a young lady who spoke very good English. In fact, she was English and had gotten left behind in Paris when her Jewish parents took off for England. She was living with a French family who had "adopted" her. She invited all of us to her home to meet her family. We put her on the front seat next to Pat, who had rank and was in charge of the rest of us, and she showed us how to get to her place.

Her "father" had been headwaiter in a large French restaurant. He showed us the trousers he had worn before the war. They were about size 48. He was about size 36 now thanks to food rationing. He had put away a bottle of wine for just such an occasion. He got it out, and I learned a new

French word that translated into "very good." Pat really made the old gentleman happy when he gave him a couple of his cigars. After a few more "very goods," George and I headed for the truck where we slept like babies. The next day we had to be on our way. Before we left, Al gave the young lady cheese from a K ration that she took to work for her lunch. I wonder what ever became of these people who welcomed us into their home as liberators.

Routes of the 392nd Fighter Squadron, 367th Fighter Group Ninth Air Force

3/23/44	Leave NY on the Duchess of Bedford
4/3/44	Arrive Glasgow, Scotland
4/4/44	Stoney Cross and P-38s near Lyndhurst
7/19/44	Don and Sgt. Wakefield with Advance Echelon—St. Mere-Eglise, France
7/27/44	Carentan, France
8/14/44	Isigny, France
9/12/44	St. Quentin, France
10/28/44	Reims, France
12/1-10/44	Don and Sgt. Wakefield—Aachen, Germany
2/1/45	St. Dizier, France—P-38s to P-47s
3/16/45	Metz, France
4/9/45	Frankfort, Germany
5/8/45	VE Day, Victory in Europe
7/2/45	Camp Detroit near Reims
8/1/45	Camp Victoret near Marseilles
8/16/45	VJ Day, Victory in Japan
8/26/45	392nd leave on USS General Brooke for NY
9/12/45	Camp Shanks, NY

A Night with the MPs

The fall of 1944 we were settled into our air field near Reims, France. We had moved into a couple of bunkers near the end of the runway that a German gun crew had evacuated a few days prior to our arrival. The bunkers were well camouflaged and partially below ground. Each one was a snug little room with roof, floor, and door, with stairs leading up to ground level. There was even a little pot-bellied stove the Germans left behind.

When the weather turned bad and our pilots couldn't do much flying, we found we had time on our hands. Eight of the ten of us played bridge, so we could usually get at least one game going when we couldn't man the trucks. It was from this cozy environment I was commissioned to go to Paris on a buying trip.

I had gone down to Paris a few weeks prior to this assignment and had returned with gifts I planned to mail home for Christmas. I had picked up some prints of Paris that are framed and now hang in our home. I had also found and bought some Lalique glassware that we still display. But the gift I returned with that caught the eye of Dan and Edge was a black Persian hat that I had bought for Lindy. They asked if I would return to Paris and get a hat for each of their wives.

When I asked Sergeant Wakefield if I could take off for a couple of days to return to the city for Christmas presents for Dan and Edge, he readily consented. He warned me, though, not to get into any trouble or to get picked up the MPs.

Hitchhiking back during those times was easy. I kept my uniform jacket clean and pressed, and the patch on the left shoulder indicated I was a member of the Ninth Army Air Force, who, along with Patton's Third Army, had the

German army in retreat. The truck traffic between the port of Cherbourg and the front lines was heavy. A lot of these trucks ran through Paris, since this is where all the good roads were located. The trucks actually ran around Paris on the Red Ball Highway. All the trucks that went up front loaded had to return. The truck drivers were happy to pick up another GI so they could have someone to talk to.

I returned to the same millinery shop where I had bought Lindy's elegant little black chapeau and picked out two more that I thought Dan and Caudle's wives would like. I rode the subway back out to the outskirts of town where I picked up a ride back home. By now it was getting late in the afternoon.

A truck driven by a Black GI and loaded with jerry cans full of gasoline picked me up right away. We were headed for the front lines, which were by now all the way to Metz, France—right on the border of Germany. I learned a whole lot later that Patton had a real fight on his hands when he tried to dislodge the Germans from the well-fortified positions in and around this town. I really didn't care where we were headed as long as it was near our field outside Reims.

It soon turned dark and started to rain. What a miserable night to get dropped off and try to find a ride back up to our field, which was off the main road. I decided to stick with the truck driver and try my luck in the morning when someone could see me and my uniform and give me a ride.

"If I stay with you," I asked the Black driver, "Where do you think I could stay all night?"

"Well, man, you can't stay with me, you know. I'll drop you off at the MP station and maybe they will put you up for the night."

"I'll stick with you for now," I replied.

It wasn't long after this decision that we started to see what I thought was lightening off in the distance and the rumble of thunder. My driver soon put me straight. "That's cannon fire up ahead, man. We're getting close to the front lines." I swallowed hard and crossed my fingers. Had I made the right decision?

I got out of the truck at the MP station and explained to one of the GIs with the white arm band and white helmet that I was trying to get back to my outfit near Reims and asked if they had a place I could bed down for the night. "We've got plenty of room and we will even feed you if you're hungry," he replied. Things were starting to look better already.

The MPs had taken over a German brewery, so I not only got food to eat; I got a canteen full of beer to drink. The beer was pretty strong, and I was tired from traveling all day, so I asked them where I could curl up and sleep. "Right upstairs," the MP told me. Upstairs was nothing but a wooden floor—no cot, no mattress, no nothing. But it was dry! I found some old newspapers over in one corner that I spread over me and in a few seconds I was out like a light.

In the morning I had a good breakfast and was on my way home. The MPs stopped a jeep that was headed my way and off I went with my package under my arm.

Those MPs were really nice fellows. They never even asked to see my pass. Good thing they didn't—because I didn't have one.

My Carbine Rifle

Part of our basic training at Sheppard Field, Texas, was learning how to use the M1 rifle. I did pretty well on the rifle range and qualified as a "marksman." My early Boy Scout training came in handy. When we arrived in England on 4/4/44 we were issued the much smaller carbines, which we were told to keep near us at all times once we landed in France.

I was the youngest GI in our ten-man radio communications outfit. Sarge Wakefield, who was in charge of the ten of us, asked me to go with him as part of the advance echelon that crossed the English Channel on July 19, 1944, just six weeks after D-Day. Wearing full infantry field equipment, we took one of our three trucks and set up for business at A-10 near Carentan. My little carbine rifle was by my side.

Early in November of 1944, after supporting General Patton's dash across France, we were settled in at our field known as Juvincourt near Reims, France, when Wakefield again asked me to accompany him on detached service. We loaded up our gear in our duffel bags, threw our rifles over our shoulders, and climbed into the back of an army truck which took us up near the front, which was by now just over the hill from Aachen, Germany. Our job was to operate the radio trucks used to help our pilots communicate with the ground coordinators.

I got sick with the flu and never got out to "The Line" the entire three weeks we were there. When it was time to return, I was so glad to be going back that in my rush to leave I left my carbine under my bunk.

We got back home near Reims just before the Battle of the Bulge began on December 16, 1944. Everyone was jumpy including our CO, who decided to pull an inspection to be sure we all had our rifles in order. I didn't have one as I'd left it under my bed. There was nothing to do but try to find one. I was lucky. I found one in a ditch where some paratrooper had lost it. I prayed he didn't lose his life along with the rifle.

At the proper moment we all lined up with our rifles beside us. The CO started down the line, looking at each gun. Wouldn't you know it? When he got to mine he not only pulled the bolt to make sure it worked, he looked down the barrel, or tried to look down the barrel of my gun. Guess he couldn't believe what he saw because the barrel was full of mud. "Pull this man's pass," he shouted. "He is not getting off base until this rifle shines!"

That weekend was spent cleaning up my little carbine. Lucky me! Lucky to have found a replacement for the one I lost and lucky to have never fired a shot in anger or battle.

My Adventures with Sgt. Wakefield

I don't remember if Sgt. Wakefield (Wake) asked for a volunteer or if he appointed me to go with him as part of that Advance Echelon, but before we took off I acquired two ceramic hot plates that we were able to plug into our truck's electrical system in order to heat coffee and C rations. I put these into the truck along with three cushions from our cots that we were lucky enough to find in our hut at Stoney Cross station 452–New Forest Airfield. I threw in two wooden collapsible cots, too. We took off for the loading area in Southampton. We were bumper to bumper for miles. One spot, I jumped out of the truck and ran up to a little restaurant that was selling fish and chips. Chips turned out to be French fries.

We finally got down to the docks, where the navy lifted up our truck and dropped it into the hold of a flat-bottom ship—an LST (Landing Ship Tank). While everyone else was up above watching the crossing, I nosed around down in the hold of the ship and found a huge supply of rations the sailors had put down below for themselves. Well, when no one was looking, I grabbed about five large boxes of the stuff and slipped them into our truck.

When we finally got off the LST and onto the beach, we drove up and parked alongside a hedgerow. At one point I looked on the other side and saw a huge stack of wooden boxes. I asked Wake what was in them. He recognized the boxes as being shells for cannon. I though to myself, "Hope Jerry doesn't drop a bomb on that pile of stuff. We'd all be blown to Kingdom Come." I didn't really have much to worry about, as the air space above the beaches was controlled by our Air Force—probably our own pilots from the 392nd.

The cots and hot plates came in handy that two or three weeks that we were stuck on the beach. Wake rigged up a metal base for the hot plates and figured out a way to hang our cots from the wall of the inside of the truck using parachute harness that was in abundance all over the place. When we cracked open the navy rations, I realized the navy guys were going about their job on full stomachs. The boxes were loaded with good things to eat, especially the bacon. We had a real good thing going until one day our Communications Officer dropped by to see how we were doing and discovered we were doing better than he was. He made us take down our cots and sleep outside the truck like the rest of the guys were doing.

We finally got our orders on 27 July to move off the beaches and head for A-10 Carentan. We drove down part of the Red Ball Highway. The engineers had laid a four-inch pipeline alongside the road and were pumping gasoline up front as fast as they could to keep up with General Patton. On the highway were trucks pulling pontoons for building bridges, trucks hauling gasoline in five-gallon cans, etc. We were all headed east as fast as we could go. Wake used to drive with his left hand on the wheel and a cigarette in his right hand. That sort of scared me—especially when we started down a hill. We would all go down as fast as the truck and trailer would go so we could get up the other side without shifting gears. I rode shotgun and Wake poured it on. What a ride!

We got to A-10, and our first job was to put up the antenna at the end of the runway. The engineers had built a landing strip out of metal that they hooked together. I came close to dropping a coil of wire on Wake's foot in my eagerness to get the equipment out of the truck and get into business helping the pilots.

The second time Sgt. Wakefield and I took off from the rest of the boys was in the fall of 1944. The 367th was at Juvincourt near Reims, having arrived there on 28 October 1944. We took off in an army truck with CNS guys from the other two squadrons. We drove through Liège and kept going until we got pretty close to Aachen, Germany, where the 367th was doing ground support.

I came down with the flu and didn't do much that whole trip except stay in bed, drink lots of liquids, and take aspirin. I finally got well enough to take a shower in a building that had been used by coal miners to clean up after working down below all day. I left the building and took a short trip down the road, where I saw something I'll never forget.

I stumbled onto a military cemetery that was in full operation. I asked one of the GIs who was working there if he would show me and explain to me what was going on. Well, I found the army was very well organized in this respect. A bulldozer had dug a trench about five to six feet deep and about a city block long. Jeeps with two-wheel trailers behind would bring in dead bodies—some fully clothed, others naked, depending where they found them. The sergeant in charge would go through the dead person's wallet and remove anything that might embarrass his family.

Then he would put all personal belongings in a little cloth bag with the guy's name, rank, serial number, and address of his next of kin. All this information was found on the GI's dog tags. Next they took one dog tag and nailed it to the back of the guy's skull with two nails. The second dog tag was later nailed to the white cross they placed at the head of the grave. The bodies were all slipped into white cotton bags, then laid out nice and neat in the trench. Next day the bulldozer came and covered up the grave and the crosses were placed at the head of each man.

Needless to say, I was glad when Wake and I headed back to Juvincourt and the rest of the CNS Gang. We didn't know the Germans were getting ready to bust out on December 16 in what became known as "The Battle of the Bulge."

As I look back now on our year and a half together, I think we had a really great gang of fellows. As I remember, Sgt. Wakefield never got excited, angry, or upset. There were never any arguments about work assignments, passes to leave the base, or disagreements among the fellows. Keim was allowed to lie in his bunk all morning, and George Roman and I were allowed to get up early and set rabbit traps. We really had a pretty good time.

Around the Clock

Our squadron received high performance ratings in communications. We maintained continuous written logs of air-to-ground and air-to-air radio traffic for each mission. This initially helped us determine radio equipment performance and later became useful in locating downed aircraft on the "Missing in Action" list. We were also responsible for ground communications installations and maintenance at each new base. We had an advance echelon which moved ahead and set up as the rear echelon prepared to vacate the old field. Both echelons had similar specialists and equipment so that aircraft leaving the old base could land at the new field without interruption of ground support.

My section in the 392nd worked in two shifts. The day shift maintained the mission reports and logs and kept ground equipment in working order. The night shift handled the heavier maintenance load as required by the routine inspection schedule and the day's combat missions.

A memorable part of my communications assignment was the setup and handling of our homing station. This was staffed by a special group of men from each of the squadron communications sections. All had taken extra training at Madison, Wisconsin. Before D-Day, this group was stationed on the south coast of England to assist in directing aircraft back from missions over the continent.

The Grand Hotel—Winter of 1944

In his book *Citizen Soldiers: The U.S. Army from the Normandy Beaches to the Bulge to the Surrender of Germany*, Stephen Ambrose wrote, "On the eve of the opening action in the greatest battle the U.S. Army has ever fought, not a single soldier in that Army had the slightest sense of what was about to happen." He was right.

I was in France just north of Paris listening to the BBC radio and getting ready for my first Christmas away from home. We had heard that Glenn Miller and his band were crossing the English Channel to be in Paris for the Christmas season.

"Glenn Miller's Band is performing at the Grand Hotel in Paris!" Al and I both excitedly exclaimed to Sergeant Wakefield. "Could we both leave camp at the same time and hitchhike down to hear them play? We won't get into any trouble and we both promise to return before the weather clears up and our planes start to fly again."

How could Wakefield say no to a couple of young guys who had been listening to Glenn Miller music since meeting and joining up with the 367th Fighter Group in Sacramento, California? Glenn's music had started to be played on every

Glenn Miller

jukebox in the States long before either of us got drafted and entered the Army Air Force.

Glenn had volunteered to enter the U.S. Air Force on November 23, 1942. He chose to take himself and his band overseas, to where he could do the most good for the morale of the fighting men. So on June 18, 1944, the band set sail for the ETO on the *Queen Mary*. After only five and a half months in England, Glenn was permitted to take the band to Paris, France, which had been liberated on August 25, 1944.

So on December 14, Glenn took off for Paris by plane, and his band left by boat to cross the English channel to start their engagement at the Grand Hotel.

Well, Al and I did get to leave base and were there the next day! We wound up in the Mirror Room of the Grand Hotel. Ray McKinley was directing the band. We didn't see

Glenn Miller that day. No one knew what had happened to him, but Al and I were really enjoying the music. "In the Mood," "String of Pearls," and "Jersey Bounce" had us dancing in the aisles. The few WACs that were there didn't have a chance to sit down between numbers. And some of those GIs could really jitterbug.

Finally during a break someone yelled out "Attention!" We all jumped to our feet and turned to see a bunch of "brass" enter the room. And guess who we all saluted as he entered the room. It was General Eisenhower himself!

"And he passed our table by only a couple of feet," we told the rest of the CNS Gang when we got back to camp. "We sure were glad they weren't checking for passes," we told the fellows. "Sarge hadn't issued us one."

It wasn't until later that we learned Miller's plane had disappeared over the English Channel. To this day, no trace of it has ever been found.

Our feeling of safety and security changed abruptly on December 16. Bad flying weather had plagued us most of December. "We won't bother them if they won't bother us" was the sentiment at the front. Hitler had had other ideas as early as September. He knew Germany would never win the war by defending the Siegfried Line and then the Rhine River. His only chance was to win a lightning victory in the West. That's when all Hell broke loose! The Battle of the Bulge was just beginning.

Nearly a half century later, I returned to the Grand Hotel when Lindy and I toured Europe with our friends. On August 20, 1991, Floyd Esche and I asked the manager in charge of the hotel if the Mirror Room still existed. He assured us it does and is visited by former GIs every year. All have fond memories of this place where we danced and dreamed of getting home to our loved ones.

Soldiers Bring Christmas Cheer to French Orphans

This article in the *Post-Tribune*, La Salle, Illinois, appeared in 1945 with Don Huling's picture.

U.S. soldiers stationed in France who entertained a group of French children from an orphanage at a Christmas party overseas were reminded in many ways of their own holiday parties enjoyed in the States.

One La Salle soldier who felt that way was Cpl. Donald Huling (pictured above), who in a letter to his wife, the former Lindy Marshall, daughter of Dr. and Mrs. E. G. Marshall, Gunn Avenue, La Salle, expressed the thrill they experienced in entertaining them.

He wrote, "It was always an important time when Santa came to Sunday school and today wasn't any different from one of those Sunday school Christmas parties we used to have.

"I remember those vesper services with Johnny Wacker and I serving as flag bearers at the Congregational Church and I remember Rev. McClary too."

Following the service the soldiers invited the children to the camp for supper. They were taken in GI trucks and served in the mess hall, about 40 of them, all under the age of eight.

"Any soldier who wanted one could have one. It looked nice to see some big fellow carrying a little girl or boy around in his arms. They all seemed to go for our white bread, and, having eaten French bread, I can easily understand why.

"Later we gathered at the theatre where we enjoyed a program put on by the children. There was a GI interpreter and I'll never forget the songs those children sang for us. Although none of them was over eight years of age, many being much younger, they sang perfect two-part harmony. We surely did applaud them.

"Following the show we took the children to the Red Cross where each was presented with a red bag full of candy donated by the boys. At the end of the day we loaded them back into the trucks and took them home. We had just as much fun as they did."

Cpl. Huling arrived overseas in April of last year and for a time was stationed in England, later going to France where he has since been stationed. He is a son of Mr. and Mrs. Thurman Huling, 744 Marquette St., La Salle.

Transition from Army Life to Civilian Life

My transition from Army life to civilian life was fast. I had been in the Army Air Force since my nineteenth birthday on February 15, 1943. After basic training, radio school, getting married, joining the 367th Fighter Group in California, shipping overseas to England, crossing the English Channel while the troops were still on the beaches, racing across France with General Patton hot on the heels of Hitler's Nazi troops, entering Germany in the spring of 1945, returning to southern France to board a ship headed for Japan, then listening to the astonishing news that the war was over after we dropped two A-bombs on Japan—I was ready to come home!

The ship that was to take us through the Suez Canal headed in the opposite direction. I still remember seeing the Statue of Liberty in New York Harbor after getting across the Atlantic in record time. We disembarked to Camp Shanks and lined up to call home to our loved ones. We had left France in such a hurry that no one had been able to contact their parents and wives that we were coming home. I finally got to a phone the next morning and contacted Lindy, who was teaching school out in the country. We made plans to meet in Chicago as soon as I got back to Rockford, Illinois, where I was scheduled to get my Honorable Discharge.

I found the hotel where I was finally able to hold Lindy in my arms again. We had been married for two and a half years but had not been able to spend much time together.

The army folks at Camp Grant were not set up yet to handle all the GIs pouring back home from overseas, so they sent me home for a month. I got a lot done during this period of transition. Lindy and I returned to Chicago to purchase civilian clothes. I felt strange and Lindy says I looked strange in the suit, coat and hat I bought. The army issued us a lapel pin we wore on our suit coat that identified us as former service personnel. We called it the Ruptured Duck. Why it got that name I don't know. I lost my original pin but was able to buy one in Naples, Florida, that is now part of my WWII display. I still wore my Army heavy rimmed glasses, and my hair had not grown out from the crew cut I had gotten in anticipation of heading for Japan.

I drove down to the University of Illinois and enrolled in the Navy engineering program that started the day after I received my discharge from the Army Air Force. It was the day after Halloween, 1945. I was a civilian again.

Army Presidential Unit Citation

The Army Presidential Unit Citation with bronze oak leaf cluster that I display at the top of my WW II Awards Plaque was presented to the 367th Fighter Group for two outstanding air battles flown by the pilots of all three squadrons.

The first citation reads as follows:

For its outstanding achievements on August 25, 1944, the 367th Fighter Group received the Army Presidential Unit Citation that stressed the Pilots gallantry in action and the ground crews professional support skills.

The Bronze Oak Leaf Cluster was awarded for the March 19, 1945, nearly flawless raid on the Castle Headquarters of Field Marshall Albert Kesselring, German Commander in Chief, West.

The details of each of the above events are found in *The Dynamite Gang—The 367th Fighter Group in World War II* by Richard Groh.

The event of August 25, 1944, took place near an enemy airfield near Laon, France, which is north of Paris. Our pilots were flying the Lockheed P-38s they found parked on the runway at Stoney Cross, England, in April, 1944. They had been in a

dogfight on August 22 in which they shot down fourteen enemy planes for the loss of one man. They had returned on the 25th to do more damage to the enemy airfield. Each squadron had its own target, but stayed in easy support distance of the others. This was the same air battle in which Captain Larry Blumer shot down five enemy fighters to become an Ace in one day.

Jubilant over their morning's work, the pilots went out that afternoon to strafe enemy airfields in Southern France. The ground crew's professional support skills made this turnaround possible. Maintenance and armament personnel stayed on the flight line while planes were away on mission. They sprang into action as soon as the planes over Northern France returned to base. Communication personnel manned their three trucks whenever a mission was scheduled and stayed at their posts round the clock, if necessary.

The commendation cited the group for bombing three airfields in France and engaging more than fifty enemy aircraft in combat, destroying twenty-five and damaging seventeen. On the same day, said the citation, the pilots flew an additional fighter sweep 900 miles without external tanks or bombs to Dijon, France, to support Allied landings in Southern France. There they accounted for sixteen German Ju 52 transport planes in strafing attacks.

The almost total destruction of Kesselring's Castle Headquarters at Ziegenburg, a small town near Bad Nauheim, Germany, took place on March 19, 1945. The 367th Fighter Group, who had been flying P-47s since February 1945, was assigned this task. The group flew this mission only three days after arriving at Jarney near Metz, France. Kesselring had won Hitler's favor with his stubborn defense of the Italian Peninsula, and the Fuehrer hoped he could accomplish a similar feat in Western Germany.

So, the 367th MISSION—Clobber the target and deprive Kesselring of his communications. Then the attack across the Rhine would take place, and the German commander would have no way of knowing what was going on and could not shift reserves or anything else.

Lieutenant Diefendorf and his wingman, Captain John C. Adams of the 392nd Squadron, hit the Castle first. "We had 8–11-second-delay fuses for the reinforced concrete, and went in low," said Diefendorf. "I picked the front door of the Castle as my aiming point. I fired a long burst of gunfire to record the target on my gun camera, then pickled my bombs and pulled off at 500 feet. I saw my 1000-pounders go off right in the front door, direct hits."

The 394th planes came in next. They carried two 1000-pound demolition bombs that they dropped on the smoldering ruins. The 393rd finished the job by dropping napalm that caused the entire area to burst into flames.

MISSION ACCOMPLISHED.

The author of *The Dynamite Gang* paid tribute to the ground crews as well as the pilots:

> None of the 367th's accomplishments would have been possible without the efforts of a small army of support personnel. Welders, cooks, adjutants, painters, mechanics, sheet metal men, armorers, dentists, surgeons, clerks, bomb disposal experts, and a host of other specialists were required to keep the pilots and planes in the air. These men never had the satisfaction of dropping bombs or firing on an enemy target, but they were nonetheless dedicated to their jobs and to the pilots. With a little griping and a lot of good humor, they withstood the privations of pup tents, C-rations, powdered eggs, parts shortages, and long hours on the flight line without shelter from sun or snow. They were hardworking, resourceful men who met problems head-on and solved them. Whether they operated a typewriter or loaded ammunition, they did all they could to make each mission pay maximum dividends at minimum cost.

367th Fighter Group Association

In 1979 Peter R. Moody published *The 367th Fighter Group in World War II,* an excellent history that reflected on the deeper, more enduring meaning of the group's outstanding combat record:

> The fact that over one thousand men, militarily inexperienced and strangers to each other, could organize, train, and within a short time achieve a notable combat record against the enemy is a remarkable tribute to our nation and to the men themselves. For these thousand men, from diverse backgrounds, education, creeds and beliefs, did have a mutual element. They were all Americans, loved their country, and were willing to sacrifice, to submit self to service.
>
> From this common bond they were sufficiently flexible and strong enough to forge a spirit and a pride that made the 367th, at least for them, unique. It was their unit. Proof lies in the fact that, several years after the war and after those thousand men had long separated to their individual aspirations and careers, the 367th Fighter Group Association was formed and reunions are being held regularly. Pride and devotion to the unit remain.
>
> Men don't share the hardships and sacrifices of military service without benefit. Our gain has been mutual. It is principally of the mind and heart. It includes ruggedness, tolerance, patience and friendship.

The ten members of the CNS Gang were so eager to get on with our lives that we lost touch with each other for many years. My first contact with any member of the Gang was in 1984. Lindy and I attended a reunion of the non-commissioned 367th personnel in Washington, DC, where we met Pat Tramontozzi, who had attended other reunions of this group.

Then in 1991 all of us except Wakefield, Abeta and Keim got together in Memphis, Tennessee. This included Edge, Dan, Grif, Pat, Andy, George and me. We all did it again in 1992, including Al Keim, out in Oklahoma City, Oklahoma. Andy Cummins and George Roman hosted smaller get-togethers in their homes. We didn't attend a big one until 1999, when those of us who were still able got together in Pittsburgh, Pennsylvania.

PART II

WAR ERA STORIES BY PAUL HULING

Fireman Second Class P.T. Huling

The Goldbricks

After boot camp at Great Lakes Naval Training Center, I found myself sort of hung up at OGU (Out-Going Units). OGU is where you are assigned your ship, or duty. Most companies arriving at OGU were sent in one or two groups to some large ships needing replacements. A company was 120 sailors.

But my Company #585 was being picked at. Only a few of us were assigned duty each day, if at all, and we were eager to get going someplace, anyplace but OGU!

OGU was a huge building the size of eight regulation basketball courts side by side with space at each end to spare. This one room housed thousands of us in bunks three high. And what do you do with thousands of antsy sailors all day? You try to find something for them to do!

So the day went like this. Each morning we would stand in line for breakfast. We would be in line before the chow hall opened to be sure there was someone to feed when the hall did open. Then we would walk back to OGU and stand in line for muster. We each had an assigned spot within our company, in alphabetical order. The boatswain in charge would walk along the line and read off names of the person he was in front of. When he got to you, the name he called out better be you or someone was missing and in trouble. One always stood muster.

But immediately following the boatswain, maybe two or three men behind, was the duty officer with a list like: garbage detail, kitchen crew, yard pick-up, toilet cleaner, sweeper . . . you get the idea. This guy was dreaded.

The sailor next to me was David Jones. Dave and I were always as close as H can get to J in everything we had to stand in line for . . . like shots. Well, we both got the same idea at the same time: as soon as we called out our name to the boatswain to verify we were there, we would wait for him to look at his list of names, then we would glance at the duty officer and when he was writing down the name of whomever he had just assigned a duty, Dave and I would take one step back and walk behind the line of sailors whose names started with H, G, F, etc., as though we were in the crew the duty officer had just assigned. Boy, did this work slick!

So Dave and I became "goldbricks." No duty. All we had to do was avoid being caught. That meant we had to walk as though we were on an assignment. Sometimes we would "fall in" with a detail going someplace, then "fall out" before we got to that place. In short order we knew the routines of every work detail and the back ways around the whole camp area and which detail went to chow first so we could fall in the chow line with them and not be detected as goldbricks.

Well, one day we almost got caught because we were sitting under a tree when we should have been walking. So we walked and walked and walked so far away from OGU that we were at a gunnery training station miles from our own chow hall. As luck would have it, there was a group approaching their chow hall that must have just been released from a training class, so we fell in at the end of their line and whizzed right through the chow line. What a great meal! What a nice quiet cafeteria! What a pleasant atmosphere! Even the air was cleaner in this section of the Great Lakes Naval Training Center, as it overlooked Lake Michigan. And everyone was friendly besides. They never guessed we were goldbricks.

So the next day, and the next, etc., Dave and I journeyed to our new-found camp for lunch and for dinner, too. What a life!

Then one day we returned to OGU after lunch and someone whose name began with G or J or something told me my name was posted because I wasn't in line after muster to receive a message. Uh-oh, I didn't think the duty officer carried messages, too!

Dave and I quickly gathered our wits. "If I report at the desk for a message the duty officer will ask me where I was, regardless of the message. And what is the message? It may be important!" So we worked out a plan.

We walked back to the gunnery camp cafeteria. We walked in the back door of the kitchen and asked to speak with the chief cook. We told him everything. We were in trouble. And the reason we were in trouble was because his food was so good. And would he put us to work in his galley, right now, and cover for us at OGU saying we worked for him that day?

First, he complimented us on our neat trickery, then our honesty. Then he said he'd consider it after we worked awhile.

I was assigned salads. Dave was pastries. We worked hard. It felt good to be doing something, especially something clean, and fun, and good to eat!

The chief cook called OGU and asked for the duty officer. He asked the duty officer to assign us his cafeteria again tomorrow, that by some error maybe on the duty officer's part, we had been assigned to his cafeteria and he was so pleased with us he wanted us back. It worked! Then the dear old chief cook asked the duty officer what my message was because he couldn't spare me to walk back to the desk until the chow hall was cleaned up. The message was that "Rogers Rangers" wanted me to volunteer for duty. Survival rate of Rogers Rangers, sailors who went ashore before the Marines to study and prepare a beach, was about 10 percent. I didn't feel called to volunteer; I wanted to serve salads.

The next day the chief cook called the duty officer again and asked that we be assigned to his barracks until our permanent assignment was made because he liked us so well. This was done. Dave and I had wonderful duty until we were assigned PC 552 together. Our hours were few, our duty interesting and light . . . the heavy, dirty work was done by work groups sent out from OGU. And we didn't have to stand in lines!

Choir Company 585

The line ". . . for those in peril on the sea" is from "Eternal Father, Strong to Save," the U.S. Navy Hymn. It was the theme hymn for the Bluejacket Choir in 1945, in which I sang from April through June. Each radio show we performed on CBS closed with the Navy Hymn. It was the first song we sang together as a choir, when Choir Company 585 was formed in Great Lakes Naval Training Center, and the last song we sang together when we graduated from boot camp and were sent to our assignments around the world.

On V-E Day, Company 585 was awakened by our Company Commander, E. J. Witte, about 2 A.M. It was to be a long, long day. Before broadcasting, live, at 6 A.M., we had marched two miles, rehearsed, and eaten breakfast. By 6 P.M. we had performed twice more on CBS radio and were marching our weary way back to our barracks . . . singing all the way. A senator from the State of Illinois awarded Choir Company 585 a citation for outstanding performance that day.

But the most memorable thing that happened that day for me was not what we had done to lift the spirits of a country which had ended the war in Europe; it was lunch.

Sometime during the day we were queued for lunch. It had to be served fast because we had more rehearsals for more broadcasts. We were given "special privilege," in other words, we went to the head of the line at the huge chow hall at the main camp. It was a brick building with a very high ceiling and windows all around except the serving center. It was already full of sailors eating when we fell in line. Half of us went to the left, and half to the right side serving lines, which meant there was about eighty feet between the two lines.

And then our choir director stood halfway between the two lines, raised his hands, gave us the pitch and directed us to sing very, very softly: "Eternal Father, Strong to Save."

The walls were plastered, the ceiling plastered, the floor tiled, the galley full of dish noise, pots and pans rattling, sailors clanking their table service on their metal trays as they talked and ate. Not good acoustics?

But the sound of the music, so soft, so gentle, drifted across the expanse and permeated all other noises. It was like a prayer, first the sailors, then the servers, and then the galley fell silent while the choir sang. The sound of our voices was like a pipe organ playing in a huge cathedral, an organ that sang words that clearly entered each ear, yet echoed each tone.

When we finished, there was silence. No one moved, spoke, or ate. Then, one of the servers on the chow line asked, "Could you sing more?" Yes, we could sing happy, happy marching tunes as we moved through the line. The noise resumed slowly and the music died down slowly as we were served and sat to eat.

Of all the songs, of all the times we sang for unknown quantities of people through our broadcasts around the world, I know we captured one audience, and ourselves, and I pray "for those in peril on the sea," who were still fighting for us.

How to Overcome Seasickness

"Just relax, don't fight it!" Charlie, the old salt in the engine room, told me as I "tossed my cookies" in a bucket I always carried during rough days at sea.

"Sure, easy for you to say. You've never been seasick. How should you know how to overcome it when you're never sick?" I responded.

"Well, at least I know where straight up is, and that's all I need to know," he said.

Now, that got me to thinking. Maybe if I knew where straight up was, I would settle down and stop being sick. What I had been doing was locking my arms around some pipes that ran up the bulkhead behind my stool which sat at the engine controls on the front of one of the main engines.

"Maybe," I thought, "instead of locking myself into the motion of the ship I should 'float' in a vertical position. Would that work?"

So I crawled into the gear locker and retrieved a plumb bob. I suspended the plumb bob from an overhead pipe. The only place with enough space for the plumb bob was between the two main engines; you see, my ship, PC 552, not only rocked from side to side, it also pitched from fore to aft because of its smallness.

So I stood in front of the plumb bob and did what it told me to do. Only, funny thing, the plumb bob was attached to the ceiling and I was attached on the floor, which meant that when the plumb bob appeared to move left, I had to lean right so I would stand parallel to the string attached to the plumb bob. This took a lot of coordination as the string appeared to be going in circles. So I would lean forward, sway to the right, lean backwards, sway to the left, and so on, following the string.

I can't say it did any good. I had not yet completed my test before Charlie, the old salt, grabbed my bucket and commenced to throw up in it. He was green! He looked awful! He was mad! I was laughing! He grabbed the plumb bob and pulled it down.

The rest of that shift I watched both main engines as Charlie had commanded. It seems he had to climb down into the bilge to check on something down there and didn't come back for a long time.

"Don't stand engine watch with Huling," Charlie used to say. "He'll make you sick!"

I never overcame seasickness but I know one method that didn't work. Just ask Charlie.

My Room

Of all the rooms I've lived in, in my life, there is one I sometimes think of as possibly being a dream rather than reality. The room was 12 feet by 12 feet by 9 feet in size. The walls were painted white, the floor painted grey, the ceiling was white except for all sorts of pipes, lights, and ducts painted various colors, which effectively lowered the ceiling to about 8 feet. One used a ladder to lower oneself into this room and the same ladder to exit.

At times this room became somewhat crowded with people. You see, eighteen of us lived in this room with all our belongings. Hopefully all eighteen were never present at the same time, because there wasn't space between our beds for that many to stand, let alone sit. But there were no chairs to sit on, anyway. We generally rotated our time in this room. Although the lights were seldom out, we, of course, slept there, too.

This "room" was really my quarters aboard U.S. Navy

PC 552

ship PC 552. PC stands for Patrol Craft. The ship had no official Navy name because it was too small, so we named it, "The Pig-Iron Bastard," because the deck tended to break open along its welded seams when in heavy storms.

Our mission was to chase submarines. Well, not really chase them, because in a speed race we lost, but to keep them underwater where we had a chance at survival one way or another.

But back to the spacious quarters this story is about. When one runs the calculations on cubic feet per person, one finds that our quarters were too crowded for comfort. Yet we survived. Most of us were between 18 and 22 years old. The cook was maybe 24. We were all nice to him and he fed us well. We encouraged lights out when he slept so we could take the keys for the galley, which he hung on his bunk chain. (He wanted to be able to say he couldn't see who took the keys should regulations be followed.) I guess I should mention he was black, as were five others in this compartment. Our ship was too small to segregate. President Harry Truman had established an experimental non-segregation policy for some small ships and we were one. The only moment of apprehension I ever had about racism was one day when I exclaimed, "Oh, boy!" to some exaggerated comment made to me by one of the blacks and he asked, "Did you just call me Boy?"

"No. What's wrong?" I replied.

First he hesitated, and then he laughed and said, "Some of you Yankees don't know enough about us to be prejudiced, do you?"

We remained friends. Over the months I learned more about how simple words can cut to the soul. I tried to break myself of that expression and any other that could hurt. By forced living close together, I learned more about love than of hate.

Things ran smoothly in our quarters until 1) there was a battle stations alarm; 2) the room wasn't immaculately clean, plus everyone in it; 3) when the sea was very rough (we once listed, that's rocked in English, 47° in a very rough sea); and 4) when some sailor on the top bunk got sea-sick for one reason or the other. There was one thing worse: 5) when all 4 of the above happened at the same time. And for me, personally, whenever the sound of the engines changed, I was wide awake even when I didn't need to be, as the engines were in my care, my ticket back to land.

My dad asked me what kept me in my bunk when the ship was floundering in the sea. I assured him I wasn't in my bunk. On days like that, I was peacefully wedged between two running 1200 HP engines with my bucket. Don't ask too many questions about my bucket.

The day I left the ship there remained only 37 sailors of the 68 that comprised the wartime quota. It would seem that both those leaving and those left behind would rejoice to have more space, but what we had shared with each other, for our country, gave good-byes a feeling of emptiness that is indescribable.

Midnight Requisitions

"When I get back, I want to see this entire ship repainted and ready to sail," said the ship's captain. Wow, that seemed like a big order to me because the ship was such a mess we couldn't even sleep on board.

The ship, PC 552, had just returned from duty in the Azores, off the coast of France. Germany had been defeated while I was in boot-camp and I had been assigned to PC 552 while it was on its way to the war still raging with Japan. But PC 552 needed all engines overhauled. It also needed new insulation to withstand the heat of the Pacific war zone. Repairs were needed under the ship which required the ship to be lifted into dry-dock.

The repairs would take about a month at the Charleston, South Carolina, shipyard, so the captain took his first home leave while the ship was removed from his command at the shipyard. He would be gone thirty days.

Shipyard workers were everywhere aboard PC 552. Some were burning holes in the deck so the large diesel engines could be lifted out, others were tearing out old cork insulation throughout the entire inside of the ship, then replacing it with new fiberglass type insulation. Others were using air hammers on the bottom, making it impossible to hear. All the seamen assigned to PC 552 were hanging over the side of the ship, in the hot sun, scraping paint with air hammers, while the firemen, that's me, tried to clean the engine room aluminum deck plates. Action was everywhere.

By the third week the ship was being reassembled and was back in the water. The shipyard had painted the bottom up to the water line. But inside the engine room was a mess; weld slag, weld burns, smoke, grease, handprints, and trash were everywhere. We firemen had had a pretty easy time of it while shipyard workers had torn apart and reassembled the entire engine room and while the seamen had sweat out the hot sun. We had made good progress scraping the hull and superstructure of the ship. But now we had the huge mess and only one week to straighten it out if we hoped to meet the captain's orders. And the crew living quarters, while empty of bunks and lockers and sporting new insulation on the bulkheads (walls), still needed to be painted before replacing the furnishings. We, the crew, decided the living quarters were both the seamen's and firemen's responsibility to paint. We dreaded that.

Now comes the part of the story where I hope the statute of limitations has expired. Somehow, somewhere, my shipmate Al and I came up with the idea that a paint sprayer would really be handy. We had been issued gallons and gallons of paint in five-gallon containers, and a huge box of paint brushes. Neither Al nor I liked to paint, especially with a brush. We spent hours trying to figure out ways to escape the task before us. Al and I had gone through boot-camp together and had become close friends, so we were free to dream up all sorts of ideas. Al figured a way to make our dream come true.

One night Al came and woke me up in the middle of the night and said, "Come with me." Al had the keys to a Navy panel truck. Where he got them I don't know. He was not licensed, as far as I knew, to drive a Navy vehicle, but off we went.

"Where are we going?" I asked.

"To the paint shack," said Al. "I have the keys for that, too." I didn't ask any questions then, but later Al told me he had spent a week being nice to a shipyard worker who worked in the paint shack and had talked him into letting Al open the shack early the next morning so Al could pick up the red, yellow, and blue paint we needed to paint water, air, and fuel lines. Well, we were early all right; it was about 0200 (2 A.M.).

First we selected a five-gallon paint sprayer, one that would attach right on top of the cans of paint waiting for us. Then we selected a nice new spray gun. Next we needed enough hose to reach from the engine room bilge, where we would hide the sprayer, to the bow and fantail of the ship—a lot of hose; the ship was 187 feet long. We unloaded all this stuff to the bilge of the ship. We acted very casual so none of the yard workers would suspect we were doing anything we weren't supposed to be doing.

Next morning Al did as he had promised, got more paint and returned the truck. All day long we worked to hook up the sprayer and threaded the hoses inside the ship all the way to the bow. By nightfall the entire inside of the ship had been sprayed a nice white coat. The lockers and bunks could be reinstalled anytime now but we would remain on the base because of the strong paint smell. The officers aboard the ship were in some state of shock. They couldn't ask, and we couldn't tell. They decided they would "assume" the equipment was always part of the ship, or that the yard workers had "forgotten" to remove it. Al and I decided that same thing! The officers never looked for the equipment and we never showed it to them.

The next day the skipper came walking down the pier

looking for his ship. It had been his home for over four years, but he walked right past the gangway. Then he saw "PC 552" on the bow and took a second, long, long look. As he saluted to board the ship he was greeted by a "Wet Paint" sign. His officer subordinates warned him not to touch anything. His eyes were wide in disbelief.

"I was only kidding," he said.

The next day we stood muster on board PC 552 for the first time since it had gone into dock. We would live another month in the barracks while the ship was on shakedown cruises and reloaded with supplies, etc. But during that month, the war in Japan ended (August 1945) and the skipper told us one morning that our orders had changed: we would stay in the Atlantic. That meant the ship was the wrong color; Atlantic ships are dark gray, Pacific ships are lighter blue. We had painted for the Pacific. But no worry. The Skipper made it a point to announce he was going on a three-day liberty. When he returned the ship was ready for the Atlantic with wet paint signs to greet him again.

We never returned the equipment, and once while at sea the long stretch of hoses helped save us from drifting to Europe . . . but that's another story.

My First Visit to NYC

It was a Sunday afternoon in late October, 1945, when my shipmate Howard and I decided it was time to journey over to New York City and see the sights.

Our ship, PC 552, was docked on Staten Island. We had arrived just days before. We had sailed from Charleston, South Carolina, around Cape Hatteras. I don't recall how sick Howard had been on that trip around the cape, but I do remember it was a couple of days before I felt like a human being again. Other shipmates had already gone ashore to NYC and told us how easy it was to get there, so Howard and I took off to see the city as a couple of boots from the Midwest might do.

The first thing I noticed was that the ferry boat from Staten Island seemed to travel much faster than our Navy ship that was supposed to be able to chase submarines. (I later found out that in order to chase subs, we had to keep them underwater where they couldn't travel as fast as we could on top of the water; if they ever surfaced we were out of luck.)

When we got off the ferry, we found ourselves on a street full of tall dark buildings that blocked out the sun, but not the wind. It was gloomy on Wall Street on a Sunday afternoon. Not knowing where or how to take a subway, Howard and I began walking to downtown, which by our reckoning could only be about 44 short city blocks, and maybe we would find something interesting along the way. All we saw was more tall buildings, very few people, and even fewer automobiles. It seemed there were no cars in New York during the war.

And then, to our surprise a nice little 1935 Pontiac convertible coupe pulled up alongside of us, and a little man wearing a battered old hat asked if we wanted a lift. So we got in.

The little guy was neat, sort of French-looking in his hat and sport coat, and he talked with a bit of a lisp. He asked us where we were from, where we were stationed, about our ship, and although he didn't need to, I'm sure, he asked if this was our first visit to NYC.

Well, this fellow took us on a tour of NYC from the Bowery, where we started, up to Broadway and over to East River Drive, around Central Park, to Times Square, the Post

Office, Grand Central Station, the Empire State Building (with its gaping hole from where an airplane had recently crashed into the building), and finally he parked his little convertible in a parking garage where he had his own stall. What a great ride, what a nice little guy.

Then he asked us if we wanted to see his apartment, which was in the same building only a few blocks from Times Square. At this offer Howard and I began to wonder about this guy. We had heard stories about how sailors were picked up, but then this little fellow would be no match for us if he tried anything, so without speaking Howard and I sort of agreed we could see his apartment for a minute or two, but really had to be on our way soon . . . to where we didn't know, and it must have been quite obvious to the man, who had introduced himself to us but we both promptly forgot as we figured our ride would only last a few blocks.

His apartment was big! He lived alone. The living room was a corner room with windows on two sides. It was full of tables piled high with books, and he asked us if we read many books aboard ship, which we did not; however, Howard was more interested in discussing books with him than I was, so Howard asked him more about them. The man claimed he read all these books and reviewed them, sometimes writing a little . . . like on the cover jacket of the book to tell what it's about.

It was getting late, and Howard and I felt a little nervous about leaving. The nice man walked us to a small restaurant and suggested we eat there because the food was good and not too expensive. He told us, sort of to our relief, that he couldn't stay as he had a date that evening, but he gave us his phone number and asked us to call him later in the week when we had liberty and he would entertain us and dine us someplace better. We thanked him kindly, then said good-bye.

I think I remember that Howard and I did eat at the restaurant; it was nice, a little expensive for our $52.00 a month pay, and quiet.

Knowing pretty well where we were and where we were going, Howard and I had a good visit of NYC. I was most impressed by the lights, billboards, taxis, and Times Square at night. It had only been a few weeks since NYC had turned on the flashy lights after the war ended.

We got on the wrong subway to go to the Staten Island ferry and ended up on a dark and scary street in Brooklyn. It looked just like the streets we'd seen in gangster movies, and probably was.

Back on ship the "old salts" told us we had met up with a "queer" who was up to no good and we should have punched him, or worse. (Neither Howard nor I was convinced of this.) I did call the man on the phone and falsely told him we had pulled duty on ship and couldn't make it back to Long Island before sailing. But things didn't add up; we liked him.

About 1960 I took my wife to a murder mystery movie, and in it was this little man who had shown Howard and me a great afternoon of sightseeing in NYC. His name was Truman Capote, author of *Breakfast at Tiffany's* and *In Cold Blood*.

"Answer the Phone"

"Huling, you're wanted on the telephone!" yelled the sailor who was on gang watch aboard PC 552 that September day in 1945.

"Sure, we have a phone now? What are you talking about?" I replied, as my buddies laughed.

Here we were trying to tie things down readying for the first hurricane of the South Carolina season, and I was wanted on a telephone? Me? A fireman second class? The second lowest rank obtainable? I was trying not to get seasick a whole lot more than I was trying to think up pranks to play on my fellow shipmates.

But Sullivan, on gang watch, was adamant about my being wanted on the phone.

"There's a phone on pier C and someone is waiting for you! Get going, Huling, it must be important!"

As I left the ship it was pulling so hard on the lines securing it to pier A that the ship was listing badly to port side. The seamen were trying to let out more line but there was a danger; if they let out too much, the ship might rise so high on the next wave that she would end up on top of the pier or snap the lines. PC 552 was so small we normally had to climb the gangway to reach a pier, but today with the fierce wind, tide, and choppy waves, the gangway was more like a slide you'd find in a kids' playground . . . going down was steep.

I still figured it was a joke being played on me, or else the shipyard had traced some of the equipment my buddy Al and I had "borrowed" from the paint locker a few weeks before.

I thought to myself, as I pushed against the wind's force, that if it was the shipyard detectives who were after me, I would flash the documents I was carrying that said I was to report to Charleston Navy Hospital at ten hundred hours (10 A.M.) that day . . . that would throw them off! Then I'd act bold, in charge! I'd act like my big brother Don would act and pretend I was supposed to "take the bull by the horns," use my resourcefulness, and "do what was necessary to get the job done." I could handle that . . . my big brother Don had shown me how a long time ago.

When I finally found the telephone, a box attached to a light pole, there was no one around, just the phone, off the hook, hanging in the wind and rain.

I picked it up and said, "Hello," braced for a joke.

"Hello, brother Paul?" It was my big brother! I hadn't talked to Don for over two years. I thought he was still in Belgium, France, or Germany. But the war was over! Don was home! He was able to maneuver his way through a maze of telephone operators, Navy personnel, and shipyard workers, and convince them he had a brother on a ship in Charleston, South Carolina, that he desperately needed to talk to during a hurricane.

My brother Don never gives up!

There were hundreds of ships in Charleston that day. The big ones had left their berths and sailed to open sea to ride out the hurricane. All work at the shipyard was suspended except for security. Debris was flying through the air and rain was pelting me with such great force that it stung.

But that made no difference; I was talking to Don, my big brother.

Liberty in New London

My small ship was docked within easy walking distance from downtown New London, Connecticut. The year was 1945, and my Navy buddies and I were anxious to spend our first liberty in town. Six of us had gone through boot-camp together, been assigned the same ship, and hung out together. Sometimes just two or three would have liberty at the same time, but this night all six of us were together and headed for a restaurant, any restaurant, to eat something off plates instead of trays, and off a MENU! Just think, we could order what we liked best.

After close study of the menu, to be sure we considered only what we could afford, we placed our orders. The waiter was very pleasant; he might have been the owner, we thought, because he had an air of authority about him. He also may have chosen to wait on six sailors himself rather than submit a waitress to six sailors who might be troublesome, as some probably were.

After taking our orders, he just stood there as though evaluating us as a whole, or in part, but he didn't move. Our conversation slowed as we became conscious of his continued presence, so we stopped talking and looked at him expectantly.

"You all are from the Midwest, except you," he started, "and you're from the South, aren't you?"

"Yes, sir," we replied out of habit when asked a question by an officer. Our use of "sir" had also extended to people who were older than we were.

"You're new on the East Coast, aren't you?" was his next question as he looked around to survey our affirmative responses.

"And you're lookin' for some home cookin', too, aren't you?" he added, and we agreed.

"Would you allow me to make a suggestion about your orders? You have each ordered the same kind of food you are fed aboard ship, or where you come from. You probably don't know, or are afraid to try, what we, on the East Coast, consider good eating. And I'd like to make you fellows an offer. I'll serve you a meal of our specialty foods, and if you don't like it, you don't pay for it, and if you do like it, you pay only what the meals you ordered cost. Are you on? I'll give you a minute to talk it over." Then he left.

We all agreed to his plan with a "What the heck" attitude. We didn't think he was out to gyp us.

He served us crab cakes, fried clams, fried oysters with red horseradish sauce, tartar sauce, fluffy soft buns, cole slaw, coffee, and flan for dessert. Believe it or not, not one of us had ever eaten any of these things before, except possibly poor substitutes for the delicious buns he served us that night.

Six happy, contented, "East Coast" sailors gladly paid their bills as we left, each of us asking what it was that we had eaten, as he had never told us.

"Just order a submarine sandwich next time you come in, and I'll tell you all about it," he said.

Well, we were stationed in New London that entire winter. We couldn't afford to eat out much, but when we did, we couldn't wait to hit that restaurant. One night he told us he couldn't have filled our orders anyway that first night, as meat was still rationed, and he hated to tell us he was out of everything we had ordered.

I often think about this event as I order my New England clam chowder, baked beans, crab legs or lobster, and thank the man who so cleverly introduced me to New England food and hospitality.

Fuel King

When does the statute of limitations run out on things done during World War II that were not "regulation"? Can I confess now? Is it safe? I hope so. Maybe I could plead ignorance, or human error, if I'm still guilty.

While serving on PC 552 off the Atlantic Coast of New England, the complement of crew went from 64 to 37 because so many older men were discharged or transferred from the ship when the war ended. This left us younger men to run things. Most of us were 18 years old and this was our first ship. We were given a lot of responsibilities.

I was "selected" to be Fuel King. Aside from regular duties and watches, it was my job to see to it that we never ran out of potable water or diesel fuel. Each day I would check the tanks, record usage, and submit a report to the ship's captain. (We didn't have much protocol on this ship; it was too small for much separation of officers from enlisted men.) When fuel or water was needed, I just asked the skipper to call the Port Authority to get permission for us to take on fuel or water. Easily granted. I hauled out the lines and connected them to the correct connections on the pier to which we tied. Usually the distance was 20 to 30 feet. Sometimes it was hundreds; I tried to avoid taking on fuel or water when the connections were too far away.

Well, we tied up in New London, at the submarine base, and were quite low on fuel and water. The line was quite long and it was winter. All went well until the next day, when we hit very rough weather about twenty miles off shore. The ship's main engines stopped running. No power. Then the diesel-powered generators stopped running. No electricity. No electricity meant no air compressor. No air compressor meant the main engines would not start, even if we knew what was wrong, because it took compressed air to start the main engines.

The first thing the engineering officer did when he entered the engine room with his flashlight was to demonstrate how to run down the batteries used to start the diesel generators. Now we had no way to start the generators to produce the air to start the main engines. As he left us in the dark and cold engine room to solve the problem(s), he said he'd go radio for help. Ha! No electricity, no radio! So word got around that our signalman would wave his flags for help as soon as another ship could be spotted. What an assignment that was, standing out in the cold storm!

The storm raged. The war was over. All the submarines either went under to avoid the storm or sailed back to the comfortable port on the river in New London. All the other PCs went to port also. The storm lasted for three days. It was cold and sickening to bob around helplessly. Most stand-by lights discharged so all working flashlights, flares, and signals were taken to the officers' quarters. We also got hungry. And thirsty.

By the end of the second day I had verified that the fuel tanks contained water. Thirty-one men and five officers looked to me as the source of the problem. I promptly offered my resignation as Fuel King, but had no immediate takers. How could I have made such a mistake as to place water in the fuel tanks? I was not a happy sailor, and no one was happy with me.

During the second day I showed everyone how to get drinking water: On the water tank there was a petcock every few inches up the tank. To see how much water we had, I would start at the top and turn on, and off, the petcocks going down, until one produced water. I then knew how much to add for refill.

Then it occurred to me: there was one (of the three) fuel tanks that had the same arrangement to check fuel level. If I started at the bottom petcock and checked for water in the fuel, I could tell how much water I had in the fuel tanks (because water is heavier than fuel). This done I figured we had over 1,000 gallons of water in the fuel tanks. But I also discovered that if I took fuel off the top petcock, there was little or no water in it depending on how rough the sea was which kept stirring up the water and fuel.

The officers and enlisted men with rank had already figured out it was necessary to drain the fuel filters and fuel lines to all the engines because they were going to freeze solid with ice and break the system when the water expanded to ice in the confined lines. So, without telling anyone, I took a few feet of rubber hose (that's another story, where I got that hose . . .) and attached it to the top fuel level petcocks of the fuel tank and routed it to the closest diesel generator. This was three days after the batteries had been run down by the officer, so they had a little life restored. I hit the starter and the engine began to run . . . rough, but I was still able to keep it going before every officer and petty officer came scurrying down the ladder and ordered me to turn the throttle control over to the first class motor mechanic, who shouted that I should not be pumping the throttle like I was doing, but hold it steady . . . "like this." The engine promptly died and he ran down the batteries again trying to start it.

I thought they were going to throw me overboard before I could explain that I was using clean fuel with no water in it.

Some hours later there was enough battery power to start the engine again . . . only this time I was nowhere around. In fact, the motor macs hooked up all the engines to petcocks, plus the boiler so the galley would have steam power to cook, so that's where I was, drinking coffee and getting warm. They were heroes; I was in the dumps.

When we got back to the base, all the water settled to the bottom of the fuel tanks, so I opened the bottom petcocks and let the water run under the deck plates in the engine room. That area is called the bilge. Should the ship leak, which it did from time to time until we welded the holes to repair it, the bilge is where water accumulates. In the bilge is a bilge pump which pumps the water out the side of the ship through a hole.

It took me most of the day to drain all the water and get pure fuel, all of which I pumped overboard that night starting about midnight. The reason I did so was because the water (with fuel floating on top) was up to and covering the engine room deck plates. It also smelled an awful lot like fuel in the engine room. I hosed down the bilge with river water.

By morning everything was fine; no smell, no contaminated fuel.

Fine that is, until I turned in my fuel usage report the next morning for 1,200 gallons of fuel used while we were drifting about like a cork for three days.

The captain called me in and said, "Is this a mistake? 1,200 gallons?"

"No, Sir," I replied. "That's how much I drained out, mostly water."

"This is going to raise many question when it's recorded at the base," said the captain. "We can't turn this in. Where is the fuel stored?"

"Oh, it's not stored, Sir, I pumped it out last night," I replied.

"WHAT?" his voice quite raised. "We were here, in port last night! What if Harbor Patrol finds out? We'll both be court-martialed! Here we are reporting 1,200 gallons of fuel oil used when we couldn't use it. They won't care if we try to tell them it was just water called fuel."

"Well, Sir," I said, "I found out from the Fuel King next-door that submarines take on water as they use fuel, otherwise their fuel tanks would be hollow as they use fuel and they wouldn't be able to submerge. Submarines have separators to separate water from the fuel as it is routed to the engines. When a sub wants to clean out a fuel tank, it pumps water, mixed with fuel, back into the base tanks for reuse. But I couldn't pump it back so I dumped it. Mostly water, Sir."

Well, I was exonerated by the Captain and officers but sworn to secrecy about the entire incident. The Captain (and I) decided we would pad the fuel account a few gallons each day until we came up with 1,200 gallons extra. But we needn't have done that.

It wasn't long before another PC rammed into us just above the water line . . . in a fuel tank. More water entered the fuel tank. When we got to port, the Port Authority pumped out our fuel tanks right back into the system.

I never took on fuel at a submarine base again. I wasn't put on the carpet. I didn't lose my job as Fuel King. But I would have given it to anyone. And I really felt like an old "salt." After all, I had been in the Navy almost eight months already!

I hope the statute of limitations has run out.

The Day I Met the Admiral

While I was in the U.S. Navy hospital in Newport, Rhode Island, my ship, PC 552, was decommissioned in Charleston, South Carolina. I knew this because I had kept in touch with some of the crew.

My release from the hospital said I was to return to PC 552 by way of Boston. While in Boston I met a shipmate who was on his way to a new assignment on another ship. My ship no longer existed. Being conscientious, I sat in a slow-moving line in Boston to inform the assignment officer my orders were incorrect. The orders were not changed, so off I went to Charleston, to find my decommissioned ship.

Three days after arriving in Charleston I finally reached the head of the line to an assignment officer there. I told him there was no PC 552. He stamped my orders with a rubber stamp and told me to return when I was called. My assignment was still PC 552.

Before I was assigned KP duty on the base I walked down to the docks to see what ships were in Charleston, and there, at the same dock where my ship had been tied when we were there, sat another PC. Gee, it looked good to me, so I asked permission to board. The crew welcomed me warmly and asked me to stay for lunch. We swapped sea stories about PCs. They needed a fireman. I was a fireman.

It wasn't long before the ship's skipper was introduced to me. I should mention that PCs had a full complement of 37 during peacetime, 68 wartime, and this was now peacetime, 1946. For me to meet the skipper was like meeting the crew, as PCs were not very formal regulation ships. I told the skipper (whose rank was lieutenant junior grade) my story and also said I'd like to be assigned to his ship because the crew was so friendly. Besides, I knew all about the engine rooms of PCs.

Now, my rank was fireman second class. It would have taken nine promotions for me to become a lieutenant junior grade—that's how far apart we were in rank—yet this officer offered to see what he could do to get me assigned to his ship. Had I known what we were going to go through, I probably would have told the skipper to forget his offer to help.

Navy protocol is to use the chain of command to speak to superiors. For me to speak with the skipper, I should have asked a chief petty officer, who would ask an engineering officer, who would ask the lieutenant junior grade if I could speak to him. On this ship it didn't matter, but from here on, to get me assigned to this PC, protocol was important.

Accompanied by the skipper, I walked to the building where I had sat for three days and walked right past the lines of sailors awaiting assignments. We went to an officer behind a desk, obviously the superior officer in charge of those doing the assigning.

The officer in charge gave me a funny look as he welcomed the skipper. They talked. The officer in charge said he could do nothing but give us permission to speak to his superior officer.

This superior officer gave us permission to speak to his superior officer. He, in turn, granted us permission . . . and so on it went, until we had an appointment to speak to the Admiral of the Fifth Naval Fleet of the U.S. Navy. This meant the lieutenant junior grade and I had reached the top. On the chain of command, I was about to talk to an admiral, seventeen ranks higher than me! I could hardly believe it.

What guts it took for a lieutenant junior grade to stand up and speak for a lowly fireman second class! The only rank lower than a F 2/C was apprentice seaman, yet he spent days to help me be assigned to his ship. What a challenge!

It didn't work. The admiral told him I would not be in the Navy long enough to make it worthwhile for him to intervene. He warmly expressed his admiration to both of us for trying, then excused us. We saluted.

I don't remember the lieutenant junior grade's name nor the admiral's name, but one of my fondest memories—and there were very few—of the Navy was a skipper who would stand up for an enlisted man all the way to an admiral.

A Shipmate Named Roy

I had lost my ship. My ship was my home away from home, where my shipmates and I lived. I cast off the lines from the dock and waved good-bye to all my buddies, five of whom I had gone through boot camp with and to whom I felt especially close. I stood there and hoped I would catch up to them again before the ship was decommissioned in Charleston, South Carolina.

I never made it back to PC 552 before it was "put in mothballs." I spent six weeks in the Navy hospital at

Newport, Rhode Island, for hernia surgery before my new orders arrived telling me to report to a Boston Navy depot for assignment.

Of course, my new orders were to report to PC 552 even though I argued with the personnel assigning me that duty. So off I went to Charleston.

In Charleston I found long lines of sailors waiting for reassignments and realized it would be days or weeks before it would be my turn for placement.

I was happy to be assigned KP (Kitchen Police). My job was to fill the salt, pepper, and sugar containers after every meal. There were 250 of them and they had to be filled exactly right. The one thing that bothered me about the job was that the prisoners ate first. Some were German prisoners of war, the others were sailors from the brig. I generally fell in line to eat right after the prisoners as this was a perk for those on KP. When the prisoners left, we then opened the doors for the long line of sailors.

One day as I watched the line of sailors who were from the brig, hands behind their heads, marching in place, double time to make waiting more agonizing, I spotted a shipmate . . . Roy! What was he doing in the brig? I tried to catch his eye to see if it was really him and if he would recognize me. But he had the same blank expressionless look as the rest of the prisoners and seemed to be looking at nothing. Nevertheless, I looked for Roy every meal and it was always the same . . . no notice of me that I could detect.

Then one day he wasn't in line with the others. I worried about where he might be or what had happened to him, as life in the brig was well known to be terribly tough.

Back at my barracks a couple of days after missing seeing Roy, here he was, waiting for me at my bunk! It was a happy reunion. He had seen me all right but would have been punished had I said anything to him and especially if he had made any indication he knew me, or anyone.

PC 552 only had a complement of 37, and after I left 36, so we knew a lot about each other. Roy, always just Roy to me, had enlisted in the Navy at age seventeen. He never finished high school. He had been assigned PC 552 and never knew any other ship, nor did he want to. When it was near time for him to be discharged from the Navy, he decided to reenlist for six more years. Losing PC 552 changed his mind, only it was too late; he had already signed. He was crushed, heartbroken to lose HIS ship, the only ship on which he had ever served or wanted to serve. It was home to him.

It was the last day that PC 552 was still commissioned that Roy drew guard duty at the gangway. He was sad; he was upset; he was angry. He was also drunk when the ship's captain approached the ship and started to board. Roy drew his .45 caliber handgun and told the captain not to board the ship, to go away. The captain left.

Crew members quickly disarmed Roy. The captain returned with Military Police. A sad and dejected Roy was hauled off. The captain pleaded on Roy's behalf for a light sentence at the trial. It helped.

Roy and I soon became close friends. Aboard ship he was a Signalman 3 and I was a Fireman 2, not that that mattered much aboard our ship, but we had not been close enough to hang out together on liberty. Now we were close, but we were almost broke; that is, I had not been paid while in the hospital and Roy would never be paid for his brig time and was broke before he entered.

Until our reassignments, we never left the base. Each day I would come up with two quarters for the two of us to blow on whatever we could get with that, which was a lot in 1946. We could buy a beer (Coke for me as I still felt under age), cigarettes, candy bar, and a movie on the base.

Roy received his orders first. We had both tried for another PC, but it was not to be. I had a few dollars left, which I split with Roy as we parted. We would never hear from each other again.

Although PC 552 came to an end, there were bonds made between young men that will never be broken by time. I hope Roy had a good career and a happy life. He was a friend and shipmate; I'll not forget.

The War Was Over?

April, 2001:
Just the other day a U.S. submarine came up under a fishing boat and sank the fishing boat. It seems there has been a lot of fussing over this accident. Or maybe I'm just now realizing the games we used to play with submarines were dangerous! It didn't seem so at the time, but all sorts of memories are returning to me as I recall the eight months of duty I spent on PC 552 from July 1945 to March 1946.

Just think, we would have made headline news over some of the events that took place during that time! We were rammed broadside by a sister ship (twin ships of the same kind). We ran ashore (hit the beach when we weren't supposed to), were hit by a disarmed torpedo (we were the target of a U.S. sub), got stuck in the mud at a garbage dump (we had to wait for high tide to work our way out), ran out of fuel (ours was contaminated with water) and drifted for three days (no fuel, no radio, etc.). The ship was torn open at the seams during a winter storm (the seam was patched as the storm raged). And so it went.

And we never even made the news!

But we didn't sink . . . quite.

I recently called my friend Howard, who was on the ship after it was decommissioned and was towed to its final resting place. When the order to drop anchor was given, Howard told me, PC 552 dropped anchor through the deck of the tug that was holding it in place. Of course!

I'll bet there was some order attached to the record of each of us that served on PC 552 that said, "Discharge as soon as possible." Good!

Headlines we would have made in 1945 and 1946:

"Sisters Broadside Each Other"

"Navy Ship Grounded—for Day"

"Torpedo Saved by Entering Ship"

"Ship Runs Amuck in Garbage"

"Ship Does Splits"

"Anchor Stops Wrong Ship!"

Pay Attention

July 6, 1946, the same day George W. Bush was born, I was in the process of being discharged from the U.S. Navy. The orders were to eat lunch, our last Navy meal, then return at 1300 hours to pick up our discharge papers and $200 mustering-out pay, plus listen to a farewell from the Navy.

The last thing we wanted was to sit through another movie, which was what we expected to see; it would be Harry Truman sitting behind his desk reading some speech he had never read before to those of us he had never seen. We did not care to hear him extol our heroism, or whatever.

Maybe we saw Harry sitting at his desk; I don't remember. I do remember seeing another movie, but this one, for a change, was not about careful sex; it was about keeping GI insurance. It was a cartoon showing a guy painting the ball on top of a flagpole while standing on it, telling us his GI insurance would still be good if he fell. There was a form to fill out if we wanted to continue our insurance.

There were other things, like how to re-enlist in the Navy if you didn't like civilian life, how to apply to a school or an approved job, so you could use your GI Bill. There was a free magazine about WWII and the Navy, etc.

All we wanted was to get the heck out of there and go home! We didn't want forms, lectures, or any more shots.

Those of us being discharged yelled comments. Someone shouted at the guy painting the ball on the flagpole, "Look! He's doing it the Navy way!"

Just when things seemed to be totally out of control and the sailors were going to mutiny and run, an officer took the mike and said, "Just one more thing before you go!" He was shouted down. "Just one more thing," he said again, "then you can get in line one last time to pick up your discharges and MUSTERING OUT PAY!!"

"Hurrah," the sailors shouted, almost drowning him out. But I was listening as others were rising from their seats and edging for the exit doors. The officer said, amongst the flurry, "It's about joining the Navy Reserves. If you don't want to sign up, come down front before you leave and fill out the Naval Reserve form!"

Did I hear that right? There was too much noise to hear well, and he didn't repeat. I wasn't sure. . . . I wanted to go get in the mustering-out line. I wanted out of there! I wanted out of the Navy and I didn't want to come back, re-enlist, or join the Reserves.

"I'd better check," I thought. "How can I do this?"

So I went against the flow, toward the stage where

the officer stood waving at all the sailors leaving. I got his attention by shouting, "Where are the forms? I want to be sure I fill one out so I'll be in the Naval Reserve!"

"You don't NEED a form then, you only need a form if you don't want to join," he informed me.

"Oh," I said. "But can I see the form anyway?"

"Sure, buddy, they're over there, you can read it."

So I took it and filled it out. About six of us had listened, the rest were in the Naval Reserve.

TOP: **Don's last furlough, December 1943.** FRONT ROW: **Tom's friend, Don, Tom Seaton, Gerald Faletti;** BACK ROW: **John Huling, Allen Shemerhorn, Max Freudenberg, Paul Huling**

LEFT: **Ninth Army Air Force patch**

BOTTOM: **A downed B-26; Al and Don**

Winter 1944, France.

Two of our three Radio Trucks, Receiver and D/F.

Our third truck, Radio Transmitter

SUPREME HEADQUARTERS
ALLIED EXPEDITIONARY FORCE

TO ALL MEMBERS OF THE ALLIED EXPEDITIONARY FORCE:

The task which we set ourselves is finished, and the time has come for me to relinquish Combined Command.

In the name of the United States and the British Commonwealth, from whom my authority is derived, I should like to convey to you the gratitude and admiration of our two nations for the manner in which you have responded to every demand that has been made upon you. At times, conditions have been hard and the tasks to be performed arduous. No praise is too high for the manner in which you have surmounted every obstacle.

I should like, also, to add my own personal word of thanks to each one of you for the part you have played, and the contribution you have made to our joint victory.

Now that you are about to pass to other spheres of activity, I say Good-bye to you and wish you Good Luck and God-Speed.

Dwight Eisenhower

TOP: **Glenn and Nita Marshall, Agnes Huling holding Christie Haugen, Thurman Huling, 1944**

BOTTOM: **Don with Randy and Marshall Hopkins next to our 1955 Ford**

PART III

POST-WAR STORIES BY DON HULING

Teaching Grade School

I substituted for Lindy one week back in 1946. She wound up in the hospital due to a miscarriage, and I had a week's vacation from the University of Illinois, where I was working on a mechanical engineering degree. I told Lindy I thought I'd be able to handle twelve grade school kids for a week. Just tell me what to do.

Lindy prepared detailed instructions for me to follow. Twelve kids in eight grades with about six subjects per grade come to forty-eight lessons per day. The kids were in school about six hours per day, so forty-eight divided by six equals eight different subjects per hour I found out I was expected to keep juggling each day. Fortunately she had scheduled fifteen minutes of recess in each day.

The first day I kept right on schedule and was exhausted when I finally got up the hospital to report to Lindy. When she asked what subject I liked best, I told her recess. She said, "If you work things just right you might be able to let the kids stay out twenty minutes, rather than fifteen." I told her I thought I could do that. So Tuesday we had an extra five minutes to play baseball. I was getting into the groove with the kids. They enjoyed the extra time on the playground, and I told Lindy I thought the extra time was sort of an incentive for the kids to work harder once they got back into the classroom.

Lindy got back to the classroom after one week. I got back down to the university and was glad to do so. The kids learned a little that week about reading, writing, and arithmetic and a whole lot about baseball. By Friday I was really giving them incentive to learn. We played baseball all afternoon that Friday I substituted for Lindy.

Our House Trailer

I accepted a job as a trainee with the American Car and Foundry Company upon graduating from the University of Illinois as a mechanical engineer. The training program consisted of working at three of the company's plants over a period of nine months. There were five trainees from five different universities. Three of the fellows were single; "Ham" and I were married. The Hamiltons had a three-year-old daughter, while Lindy and I were anxious to get started. A house trailer seemed like the perfect answer to the housing problems we would be facing in the next few months.

We found a 21-foot trailer at the west end of Peru that we liked and could afford, so we bought it for $1800.00, with the stipulation that it would be delivered and parked in the Marshalls' driveway.

We were driving a 1935 Ford that Glenn and Thurman had found for Lindy to drive to school. The old car had a V8 engine that proved capable of pulling the trailer. Almost capable, I should say. I had Cyclops make a trailer hitch and attach it to the rear of the Ford. I still vividly remember backing the car up to the trailer and "hooking up" for the first time. We had the trailer pretty well balanced so there wasn't too much weight on the hitch. Even so, the back of the Ford sank a couple of inches—about the equivalent of two adults getting into the back seat. With my fingers crossed, I slowly pulled our "rig" out onto Gunn Avenue and headed south to Decatur, Illinois. If any of you have seen the movie *The Long, Long Trailer* starring Desi Arnaz and Lucille Ball you can imagine how I felt like Desi as impatient cars tried to get around us as we drove down old Route 51.

Before we left on our big adventure there were a couple of things we did to dress up the trailer and make it more livable.

Lindy's mother, Teta, treated it like a big doll house and made curtains for all the windows. We needed some kind of table to eat off of so I designed and built one that folded up against the closet wall. It locked in place, as I had been forewarned to secure everything while traveling. We had a couch that folded down into a double bed and two folding chairs. In the kitchen were a gas stove, an oven, and an icebox. A double bed in the little bedroom competed our outlay of furniture.

Lindy in St. Charles

We finally got down to Decatur, which was on our way to St. Charles, Missouri—our first training plant. Onalee and Larry took off for South Dakota while Lindy and I took care of Marshall and Randy. I would lock the trailer back door, but somehow Marshall always managed to get the door open. He took great pleasure telling his mom and dad how he could get into Uncle Don's trailer.

We left Decatur early in the morning and headed for St. Louis and then St. Charles. This was about a 200-mile trip, so we planned on being on the road most of the day. St. Charles is hilly, but after some pushing and pulling we finally got parked in our trailer court.

Remember I said the '35 Ford was almost capable of pulling the trailer? Well, here is the rest of the story. Lindy and I were invited to spend Thanksgiving with the Hopkins family in Decatur. Teta and Glenn drove down from La Salle, and we drove over from St. Charles. As we were crossing the Mississippi River I heard a pinging noise coming from the car. I pulled off at the first garage in Illinois. It didn't take the owner long to diagnose the problem as a broken piston connecting rod. What to do now? Lindy was pregnant and starting to show by now. The garage owner suggested I send Lindy on to Decatur on the next bus that stopped right out in front. I would wait until he could put a rebuilt motor into the Ford. So that is what we did. One advantage of driving such an old, reliable car was that rebuilt engines were readily available. And only $300.00. I was on my way in no time and was able to spend Thanksgiving Day with our family.

I'll always remember where we were when Princess Elizabeth became Queen of England. We and the Hopkinses were in St. Charles all together in our little house trailer. The couch that made into a bed served Onalee and Larry. His feet stuck out over the end. He had to keep his legs straight as there wasn't enough room to cuddle.

A few weeks later we packed up and headed for our second training plant in Huntington, West Virginia. This would be a two-day trip—provided everything went OK. Our goal was to get around Indianapolis by the end of the first day, then head for Cincinnati on the next. This whole adventure took place long before the interstate highway system was built, but US 40 and other four-lane highways proved to be our best bet. We could chug along at about 50 miles per hour and let the rest of the cars zoom past us.

We found a state park open just south of Indianapolis so we stopped for the night and slept in our own little home. An extension cord provided us with lights. The park had rest room facilities, and our little oil-burning heater kept us warm. We were as snug as two bugs in a rug.

The next day we pulled into our assigned trailer spot in

Winter 1948, Huntington, West Virginia

Huntington. The plant was in the middle of a huge order for all-welded hopper cars for the C and O Railroad. I didn't know at the time that we would be returning to Huntington to complete this 10,000-car order. Our friends the Hamiltons finally found a one-room apartment, but we felt our strategy was starting to pay off. Lindy and the baby were dong fine, I was enjoying my work, and we had a warm little home to live in those cold winter months of January, February, and March, 1948.

April found us getting ready to head for Berwick, Pennsylvania, which would be another two-day adventure. Getting our "rig" up to the Pennsylvania Turnpike was our first challenge, as there was only a two-lane highway winding north along the Ohio River. Getting through Washington, Pennsylvania, was the biggest challenge. The state highway ran right through the middle of downtown. I remember sweating out one stop light at the top of a hill. If the light turned red, I'd never get the rig started again. Wouldn't you know it—just as I got to the busy intersection the light turned red, but I didn't even slow down. I couldn't go any slower as I had the car in low gear with the throttle all the way to the floorboard. Fortunately no one coming the other directions panicked. Maybe they had seen this situation before. Anyway, they all sort of cheered me on and we kept going.

On the other side of Washington we spotted Agnes and Thurman coming up the hill as we started down. We sort of had our eyes out for each other as we knew they were heading out to the farm. My grandfather had passed away in 1947, and Grandmother and Wilbur were still living on the farm. Emijane was taking care of Grandmother—and Wilbur on the side. This arrangement worked well for the folks and everyone else that was involved. Wilbur and Emijane married and set up housekeeping after Grandmother died.

Berwick was a little town with no trailer court, so finding a place to park the trailer became top priority. I drove back and forth through the level part of town and finally spotted a vacant lot next to an old two-story house. I stopped and told my story to an elderly couple who, it turned out, owned the vacant lot. I worked out an arrangement whereby we could use their downstairs bathroom and plug into their outdoor light socket. I hooked up copper tubing to their outside faucet, dug a small septic tank system that took care of our liquid waste water, and we were in business.

The second order of business was to find a doctor and a hospital for the delivery of our first child. Lindy had had a scare back in St. Charles and the trip out from Huntington hadn't been the easiest for my very pregnant wife. But Lindy was a trooper. The doctor visited at our trailer, and Lindy remembers him telling the nurses at the hospital how we had all the comforts of home. Looking back, I'm sure my Boy Scout and Army experiences helped me make the whole thing just another big adventure. Donalyn was born July 3, 1948, in Berwick, Pennsylvania. We had a tiny bassinet for her, and Lindy tells the story of waking up and finding Donalyn blue from cold. We didn't know anything about raising kids. I think we did pretty well though, using Donalyn as our model.

The Hopkinses and Marshalls visited us in our little home. We had a picnic in the front yard. Lindy and I drove over to Easton, Pennsylvania, to visit my folks, who bought a house near the campus of Leigh University.

At the end of the training program, I was asked to return to Huntington. I had the company pull the trailer back down, as we were not sure how long we would want to live in it. We found an apartment across the street from Marshall College in Huntington and put the trailer up for sale. We got $1,000.00 for our little home that proved to be a pretty good investment monetarily, but a huge success taken from a much broader perspective.

My Years as Scoutmaster of Troop 2

We returned to La Salle in 1957. When Jamie became old enough to become a Boy Scout in 1962, I dropped out of the Illinois Valley Symphony Orchestra, which rehearsed on Monday nights in Ottawa, to become Scoutmaster of Troop 2. We met on Monday night in the basement of the First Congregational Church of La Salle, located on the corner of 5th and Joliet Streets. The basement had been improved by Len Trovero since I was a kid back in the late '30s and a member of the same troop with my pal, John Wacker. We had met in the upstairs Sunday school room back then. I devoted three years to the troop—long enough for Jamie to earn his Eagle Scout Award in 1965. I had gotten my Eagle Award in 1940 along with John Wacker.

The troop took an active part in Starved Rock Council activities that pitted the troops in such contests as cooking, life saving, compass reading, and fire building. The winter of '65 the scouts held a big get-together at Starved Rock State Park. The troop had a Klondike Derby sled we had built the previous year. The sled was driven by a driver and pulled by a five-man team. The challenge was to pull it to each of the four stations mentioned above, complete the required scouting skills, and return to base in the shortest length of time.

The first station combined fire building and cooking. We were to build a fire, boil water over it, and make instant soup. We had our own firewood, which we quickly formed into a high pyramid. When we threw the first of only two wooden matches they had allowed us into the wood pile, it burst into flames. We had learned to "Be Prepared"—we had soaked the kindling wood in gasoline! This first stop and early success put us so far ahead of the other troops, we went ahead and won a ribbon for our Troop 2 Flag.

Weekend winter camping at Ki-Sha-Wa was a challenge, a lot of hard work, and a lot of fun. Some troops never got going if the Scoutmaster tried to do everything himself. I had a young Assistant Scoutmaster who had been a scout as a kid and helped out a lot. Another requirement for a successful troop was to have a working committee of dads willing to help out when called upon. My committee helped out with paper drives and flyer distributions that raised money for the troop. We spent the money for pup tents and cooking gear. We had a closet in the church basement where we were able to store our sled, tents, and a red cooking cabinet. We took all this gear with us when we went camping.

One winter weekend we challenged Pete Loveland's Troop 1, sponsored by the Congregational Church of Peru, to a Klondike Derby. Our troop had gone out on Friday night, and when it came time to race on Saturday morning our team was dragging their behinds. Needless to say, Troop 1 beat Troop 2, but we sure had fun.

Another district activity was a scouting show held in Ottawa, where the public was invited and scouts showed off scouting skills. Troop 2 came up with the idea to show the public how to saw wood with a two-man saw. We built a sturdy sawhorse and used a six-foot section of a telephone pole. I had a stop watch I used to determine which two scouts—or members of the public—could saw through the large 12-inch diameter pole the fastest. This generated a lot of excitement and goodwill for the Boy Scout program of the Starved Rock Council.

Once we built a rope bridge inside the Hotel Kaskaskia. Men who had devoted a lot of time, effort and money to scouting were honored with the "Silver Beaver" award. Our bridge signified the relationship of boys becoming men of this caliber.

A Scoutmaster becomes a role model for the boys of his troop. A couple of our kids had no father at home, so I had to set a good example. No swearing, dirty jokes, smoking, or dangerous pranks were allowed. Every effort was made to live up to the twelve Boy Scout Laws, which are "A Scout is trustworthy, loyal, helpful, friendly, courteous, kind, obedient, cheerful, thrifty, brave, clean, and reverent." One young man who lived around the corner from our house on Kilmer Street wanted to be a patrol leader. I thought him immature but left it up to the boys whom he was to keep in line. It didn't work out for him, but I gave him the job of quartermaster, which fit his personality and disposition much better.

A city block from the church where we met was a public park. I would take the boys over there after our regular meeting of close order drill and working on advancements. I had the older scouts help the younger boys advance from Tenderfoot to Second Class to First Class whenever I could. Over at the park we played Capture the Flag. Some of the older boys got pretty good at devising diversionary actions to get the opponents' guards looking the other way as one of their gang ran in and captured the flag. This activity had stood me in good stead when, as a soldier, I had to stand night guard during basic training in the army. Some fellows were scared of the dark. Not me! I'd had too much fun as a Scout during night maneuvers and playing games.

Our Families' Camping Experiences

The first time we went camping as a family was in the spring of 1957. We were living in Gardner, Massachusetts, at the time. When I agreed to stay with Florence Stove Company until we got the garage door operation moved to Lewisburg, Tennessee, our neighbors loaned us their tent to use on the way down south. The first time we pitched it—it was an umbrella tent about six feet by six feet without a floor—we were right in the middle of Washington, DC. I had camped here in 1937 as a Boy Scout during the first International Jamboree. The next day we drove the Skyline Drive to the Great Smoky Mountains National Park, where we camped that night. The black bears kept us on our toes at this place. They loved to prowl around at night looking for food.

We got to La Salle the fall of 1957 and rented Elvira Ray's house on Marquette Street. I bought a big wall tent with a floor and front flap that made into a porch from Sears. This tent was about ten feet wide and twelve feet long and had screening in the doorway. The sides folded down halfway and there was screening at the top. Lots of ventilation. The first trip with this tent was out to Starved Rock State Park, where we really had a memorable experience.

The campground was down near the Illinois River below the Starved Rock Dam. We could see barges loaded with coal being pushed up the river and locking through the dam. After being raised about ten feet, they were ready to go on to Chicago.

We found a nice level spot to pitch our tent. I had also invested in sleeping bags and air mattresses that we inflated and got ready to bed down for the night. After supper of roasting hot dogs over our campfire and singing camp songs, we turned in a little early as it looked like it might rain.

And rain it did! The kids were all asleep, and I awoke as the storm passed overhead. Just when I thought the rain was over, it started up again. I mean the rain really came down and the wind began to blow. The tent stakes started to pull out of the rain-soaked ground, and water was getting inside the tent. I woke the family and told them we were getting out of the park! We took down the tent, folded it up water and all, and stuffed everything into our blue Ford station wagon. As I drove out of the campground, I realized everyone left down there was in serious trouble. The water was up over the road. I almost drove into a ditch trying to get out. I asked Lindy to drive while I walked in front of the car with the headlights on. I could feel the crown of the road with my bare feet. Ever so slowly we drove out as the water started to cover the floorboards. The kids nor Lindy ever let out a peep, but I bet we were all saying some prayers. Before heading for home I decided to alert the park ranger, Mr. Terry Martin, who was a family friend and went to the Congregational Church.

Mr. Martin and his wife answered the door, even though it was 4 A.M. I was dressed only in my jockey underwear which, by now, was soaking wet and rather revealing.

Terry saw immediately we had been through an ordeal and realized the rest of the campers had to be alerted and evacuated as soon as possible. He called the dam attendant, who told him the locks had been raised to let water from the upper pool flow down the river. This had let so much water flow that the campground was flooded. Terry called a wrecker truck from Piety Hill that arrived in time to pull campers out onto higher ground. When we got home we pitched the tent in our backyard and finally got everything dried out, including sleeping bags and air mattresses. A few years later the campground was relocated up on higher ground.

The Starved Rock adventure didn't stop us from enjoying the camping experience later this same year. The Marshalls, Hopkinses, and Hulings all headed out west to go camping in Estes Park, Colorado. I borrowed a one-wheel trailer from Robert Hubbard which I pulled behind the blue Ford station wagon. We put the tent and other gear in the trailer and found room for Teta and Glenn in our car and the Hopkinses' car. I even worked on the two rear tires of the wagon to be sure they would make the trip to Colorado.

On the map, I found a place out in Kansas, about halfway to the park, that looked like it might be OK for camping. We told the Hopkinses, who had Teta and Glenn with them, where to meet us. We thought we would all get together about four in the afternoon, but Lindy and I and all the kids—Marshall, Randy, Donalyn, Jamie, and Vickyle—got there a little later. I had to stop twice and replace each rear tire that had blown out. I had put inner tubes inside tubeless tires which blew out when they got too hot from driving on the hot concrete highways.

The Kansas campsite turned out to be a low spot along a river that had flooded and was full of mosquitoes. We drove up the road and all of us piled into two rooms at a cheap roadside motel. The adults got beds but the kids got the floor. No one seemed to mind, though, as we laughed and joked about the tire blowouts.

We got to Rocky Mountain National Park near Estes Park, Colorado, the next afternoon. The park had a nice lodge where Teta and Glen had reserved a room. Marshall said he wasn't feeling too good and chose to stay with his grandparents, rather than brave the elements with the rest of us.

We pitched the tent and finally got a fire started. We soon discovered boiling water wasn't very hot at these high altitudes. But we made coffee anyway. Then the wind started to blow, and it got cold. I lowered the front of the tent so it wouldn't blow away. All eight of us—the Hopkins three and the Huling five—huddled together and braved the cold. In the morning Marshall arrived back from his restful night ready to go hiking and horseback riding. He even found a garter snake he scared Lindy with. Not his mom, though. Onalee had fun showing us how cute the little critter was as it wiggled around on the leaf Marshall had found it hiding underneath. Larry drove all of us up Pikes Peak, except Teta, Lindy, and Vickyle. They had fun riding an inclined railroad up the side of the mountain. We packed up and spent the last night in a motel just outside the park. In the morning, Onalee and Lindy ate a memorable breakfast of steak, fried potatoes, and scrambled eggs. They had gotten tired of cooking and eating camp food.

Another memorable camping trip with the Hopkinses was our outing at Pokagon, Indiana. It rained Saturday night, but Sunday morning Onalee and Lindy drove back to Sturgis and delivered the Sunday papers for Marshall. Lindy started off by yelling "paper" as she left each house, but Onalee told her it wasn't necessary to wake up everyone that early. After all, she was the wife of the president of the bank, and to be seen delivering papers just didn't fit this position.

Other camping trips included outings with our closest friends, the Esches and the Robinsons. We drove to Devil's Lake in Wisconsin twice and Earlville, Illinois, which is just east of Mendota, a couple of times. There was a lake and grocery store near the Earlville campsite. We had acquired an aluminum twelve-foot boat and five horsepower motor by this time that we had fun using. We carried the boat on top of our green Dodge station wagon. The most fun was sitting around the campfire at night telling stories and singing favorite songs.

The Lake Superior trip in 1963 was the end of our family tent camping experiences. All the children were growing up. Donalyn was a senior in high school, and Jamie and Vickyle were only two and four years behind. Our campsite was in Brimley State Park on the shore of Whitefish Bay, which is at the easternmost part of Lake Superior. The day before we pitched our tent, I drove the family into Canada by way of Sault Ste. Marie. I had been up into Canada at this same spot when I was with Lloyd Schaffer and six other Eagle Scouts. I remembered a beautiful waterfall we found back then and I was able to find it again with my family.

We pitched the tent and bedded down for the night. It got cold this far north, but by now, Lindy and I had gotten wise to the comforts of sleeping in a double sleeping bag and air mattresses. We brought along our electric blanket and an extension cord and were "snug as two bugs in a rug."

The next day, Jamie and I rented a small motorboat and went fishing. And boy did we ever catch a big fish! We brought it back to camp, cleaned it, and Lindy baked it in aluminum foil over a charcoal fire. It was delicious.

I made a wooden sign that read "HULING 5." The sign identified our campsite, and when we got home to La Salle, the sign—and fish head—hung in our garage to remind us of all the fun we had on this adventure and all the earlier camping trips we had had as a family.

What Happened to the $500?

Jo Jo Cawley liked to talk. I liked to listen.

One day during my noon lunch period I met Jo Jo at the Ninth Street Pub. I always tried to have lunch there on Thursdays because this is when I'd find Jo Jo there ready to tell me a story or two about Kelly and Cawley's. Jo Jo had worked there for his Uncle Tom along with his brother Ryan. He told me he had been fired a couple of times but was always forgiven and hired back. The day this story took place was tough on the casino but wound up OK for Jo Jo.

Saturday, February 21, 1953, marked the historic raid that would turn the "Little Reno" of the La Salle world of casinos upside down. A secret raid on Kelly and Cawley's new establishment at 517 First Street had been planned with the knowledge of only a few people. At 3 P.M. on Saturday, Harlan Warren and Assistant State's Attorney Wendall Thompson were joined by Deputy Sheriffs Stanley Murray, David Monterastelli, Bernard Kleinhans, and investigator James Endtwhistle as they entered the cigar store portion of the building on the first floor. Kleinhans read the search warrant to William Brady, one of Cawley's clerks, while Thompson led the team to the second floor over the Senate portion of the layout and a gambling room over the cigar portion. Dealers and bartenders hurriedly tried to remove incriminating evidence of gambling activities.

The raiders confiscated craps tables, a roulette table,

poker tables, cards, punch boards, ticket boards, jars, and racing forms. They also confiscated the money on the poker tables and in the cashier's cage. According to Ryan Cawley, there was $500 in the book drawer at the beginning of every day. For some reason, never explained, only $20 actually got back to Ottawa that day. Here is the reason why.

Jo Jo told me his job that day had been to pick up pull tabs off the floor and put them into one of the large jars that they had originally come in. Jo Jo told me he knew about the $500 that was kept in the book drawer every day. During the raid, when no one was looking, he took the $500 and hid it under the pull tabs he had picked up off the floor. No one looked in the jar because they could see what was inside—just old pull tabs—so they thought.

When the raid was over, Jo Jo told me he simply reached into the jar, pulled out the $500, and gave it to his Uncle Tom later when things cooled off a little.

Jo Jo told me his uncle was so proud of him for his quick thinking, courage, and honesty that he was hired back that very same day.

Dr. Bang Bang

I had business in Chicago one morning so I put on a white shirt and a tie that matched my tan sport coat and slacks. My business kept me busy until after lunch, which I had at a hole-in-the-wall in the downtown business section. I didn't eat much as I was a little nervous. My business that day for Carus Chemical Company involved getting acquainted with Dr. McKenna, who worked for the Bureau of Explosives.

My assignment was to get permission from the Bureau of Explosives to ship potassium permanganate in a plastic bag. Our product carried a yellow label, which classified it as a strong oxidizing agent. Ammonium nitrate carried the same classification and had been approved to be packaged in a heavy plastic bag. I used this fact as the basis of my argument to get permission to ship our product in a similar container. Big savings to Carus were involved, as metal cans were the only way our product was being packaged and shipped. This particular meeting was set up just to get acquainted.

I found out Dr. McKenna was from Canada, and because of the difference in the value of our monies he asked me to buy him a quart of good whiskey that he would take home with him as a gift purchased by his new American acquaintance. I found a 1/5 Tennessee sour mash Jack Daniels whiskey that suited him fine. When we parted he said he would contact me and set up a date to come to La Salle and perform an experiment to determine the stability of our product.

It took me quite a while to get out of the city. I wasn't used to the volume of traffic. It seemed to me everyone was leaving at the same time. Anyway, by the time I got out of Chicago I was getting hungry, as the light lunch wasn't holding me very long. I had heard of an eating place north of Joliet called White Fence Farm that specialized in chicken. I decided to stop there, as it was right on my way home.

It was suppertime, and they were just opening. I found a parking spot and got in line. As I waited I noticed another line where people were being let in almost as quickly as they were arriving. What the heck! That's the line for me. I left the long line that was moving very slowly and walked right in with a couple that were about retirement age. They seemed to know where they were going. They did know where they were going, I found out, so I stuck right with them.

We wound up in a very nice section of the restaurant, but rather than small tables for four I found a place at a long table where about twelve of us sat. Something else was different.

No one came to take my order, but it wasn't long until the chicken started to arrive. I hadn't even seen a menu! I decided to get acquainted with the older couple I had tagged along with when we entered. Well, to my surprise I discovered I had crashed a company party. I guess the fellow at the door thought I was related to the older couple. When I told them I was from La Salle and was driving home after a meeting with Dr. McKenna, they insisted I stay and have supper with them. Their company would pick up the tab. I did leave a nice tip, however.

A few weeks later Dr. McKenna arrived at our plant in La Salle to do his experiment. I couldn't figure out how this would affect my goal of getting the permit the company wanted, but I went along with his request after getting the OK from Blouke and Paul Carus. He asked for a wooden box one foot by one foot by one foot with a bottom but without a lid. He wanted me to fill it with sawdust, which I picked up by Emil Wylepski's table saw. A handful of KMnO4 was placed in the center of the sawdust, then I gave Dr. McKenna a glass funnel with a six-inch glass tube that I got from Arno Reidies. McKenna stuck the funnel into the sawdust and poured a glass full of water down the funnel onto the potassium permanganate. Nothing happened. He told me to be patient. We left the box in the open just outside the electrician's shop and went home.

When I arrived at the plant the next day, Dutch Lipka, who had just come off the night shift, told me there had been a big BANG during the night. Jeff Struna showed me the wooden box. Not much was left. Walter Moshage told me it was a good thing we had done the experiment outside and not in "his" plant.

From that day on we all referred to Dr. McKenna as "Dr. Bang Bang"!

The "Birdie" Award
or
"What Did You Do to My Secretary?"

Bob Manahan began giving the "Birdie" award shortly after the L-P Chorus performed the show *Bye, Bye Birdie* in April of 1963. It was an award given to an outstanding performer whom he singled out for cooperating as directed, plus other attributes he needed to achieve the results he was looking for. Our son, Jamie, won the award for his performance in *Half a Sixpence*. I was in a position to honor such a person while I was working for Carus Chemical Company.

I had to do additional testing to satisfy Dr. McKenna—also known as Dr. Bang-Bang—in order to get permission to ship potassium permanganate in bags. Three of the country's largest bag manufacturers were eager to work with me if I should get such a permit. The tests specified by the Bureau included drop testing, to be sure the bags wouldn't burst if accidentally dropped, and shaking to be sure the bags wouldn't get a hole by rubbing on a wooden surface. All three manufacturers had test equipment, as they were all familiar with the Bureau's specifications.

Drop testing and shake testing were done in Wisconsin, Ohio, and finally in New Jersey. By the time we finished testing in New Jersey I felt we had an acceptable heavy plastic bag that I hoped would be approved by Dr. McKenna and the Bureau, who had their offices in lower Manhattan. I had been in touch with Dr. McKenna from the beginning of the testing and felt we had a good relationship. When he made suggestions, I listened.

All that remained to do was to write a final report and submit it to the New York office of the Bureau. This is when I needed help from a cooperative secretary. One of the bag manufacturers had an office in New York, and the head salesman I had been working with offered me the use of his private secretary to do my report. She got right to work on it and by noon I had my report, which I mailed that very day to Dr. McKenna.

I thought about this cooperative woman, and when I got back to La Salle I decided to say "thanks" in a rather unusual way. I purchased a large gold star which I applied to a plain red card. On the front I simply said:

> The Carus Chemical Company "Birdie" Award
> Presented to Ms. Jones for her outstanding cooperation with Donald J. Huling
> In producing a Report for the Bureau of Explosives

I mailed the card to her and didn't think any more about it until about a week later, when her boss—the salesman—stopped at our plant to talk with Ed Boll, our plant manager.

"What did you do to my secretary?" the salesman asked me. "Ms. Jones is like a new person."

"All I did," I told him, "was to thank her for a job well done."

"Well," the salesman said, "she has that little red card on her desk and has shown it to everyone in the office."

The moral of this story: Everyone likes to be praised.

The L-P High School Rotunda

When I went to La Salle-Peru High School, there was a five-foot-diameter hole in the upstairs floor with a railing around it called the Rotunda. This was a favorite hangout spot for a lot of us kids, especially if we were waiting for the bell to ring to go to Dr. Marshall's chemistry class. We could wave to anyone we knew on the first floor and anyone on the first floor could look up and wave to whomever they knew or saw standing close to the opening on the second floor, just outside the auditorium.

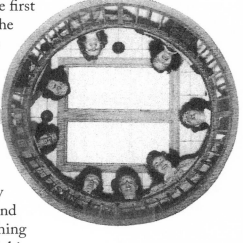

This opening is now closed. I wonder if my wife Lindy and her friend Bill Gebhardt had anything to do with the closing of this opening?

The L-P High School Rotunda
ABOVE: **in the 1940s;** BELOW: **today**

Lindy and Bill were waiting for the bell to ring so they could go to Dr. Marshall's chemistry class. The classroom was just around the corner past the boys' restroom. Well, as they were waiting,

Bill finished eating an apple he had brought to school for lunch. Different teachers patrolled the halls. This particular day Harry J. Wilmot, Dean of the Junior College, was on duty and happened to be standing directly beneath the Rotunda. Bill took aim. Lindy motioned for him not to do it, but it was too late. The apple core hit the dean right on the top of his head. He knew immediately where the missile had come from. He looked up, but all the kids had flown into Dr. Marshall's classroom. Everyone was in his or her seat looking so innocent when Harry looked in. Lindy's dad assured him everything was in order.

The other reason the Rotunda may have been closed was because it was a favorite place for kids to wave to each other. The boys liked waving up to pretty girls, especially if they were wearing short skirts and standing close to the handrail.

Open Forum

The article in the May 26, 2009, Open Forum entitled "L-P Rotunda a Place for Fond Memories" got my La Salle Rotarian friends asking me questions I couldn't answer. Many of them said they never saw the Rotunda and asked me when and why it had been removed. I had to go over to the L-P High School to learn that it was removed early in 1950 on orders from the Fire Chief. Kill joy!

The school is not sure the atractive nuisance or the good view had any input to plugging up the hole. I did find out that Gabby, as we called Bill Gebhardt, was not the only person to have fun bopping someone standing below. One person told me her dad, who went to L-P back in the forties, filled a balloon with water and had fun dropping it on someone. I haven't heard yet of anyone besides Gabby hitting the Dean of the Junior College or anyone else of this prominence with an apple core or anything else of this nature. This took courage!

The Good Samaritan

Our grandsons David and Douglas Bratton acted out the Good Samaritan story, and I videotaped them, one summer when they were spending time in La Salle. Doug was the

Jewish man traveling on a trip from Jerusalem to Jericho who was attacked by a bandit. David was the bandit and really beat him up. Then David made a quick change. He took the part of the Jewish priest who saw Doug lying there, moaning loudly, but crossed over to the other side and said, "I don't want to get involved!" Then a despised Samaritan, also played by David, came along and helped Doug get up. Then I said, "Which of these two men was a neighbor to the man that was attacked by the bandit?"

"The man who showed him mercy," both boys replied.

Then I read from the Bible what Jesus said. "Yes, now go and do the same."

I was returning to La Salle from Chicago one day and had a Good Samaritan experience. I got to La Salle on the train about two in the afternoon. I was waiting near the exit door as the train slowed down when a young lady approached the exit door in quite a state of agitation. She lived in Ottawa, Illinois, and had missed her exit from the train. She didn't know how she would get back to Ottawa. I realized her predicament and told her I would help her get back home.

I had her get into our car that I had parked at the station and drove up to our home on Bucklin Avenue. I explained to Lindy and Vickyle, who were home from school by this time, that I planned to drive this woman home. I asked Vickyle if she would ride with the lady and me. So that is what we did. We found out on the way to Ottawa that the reason she had missed getting off at her station was because she was having so much fun. Seems she had been drinking and didn't realize where she was.

There must be a moral to this story. I think there is. *Love thy neighbor as thyself.*

I think everyone in my family has, or will have, a Good Samaritan story.

A Day to Remember

It started as having fun throwing rocks at an empty plastic milk container, but it wound up as three dirty kids and an upset grandmother. Grandpa had a ball!

A couple of years ago, Lindy and I celebrated our 50th wedding anniversary (1993). We had all the children and grandchildren in La Salle to help us celebrate this joyous occasion. We all had supper one evening at the Red Door and wound up alongside the Illinois River pitching rocks to see who could throw the farthest. This planted an idea in my mind. I mentioned it to Dave Bratton, who added a little twist to it that may have contributed to the three dirty grandsons.

Lindy and I picked up Brett, Evan, and Jessie at the Indianapolis airport Saturday, July 15, 1995. Jessie flew in from Nashville, where he had spent most of the summer with Jamie and his wife, Michelle. Vickyle and Don drove up from Cincinnati with the two boys, Brett and Evan. Indianapolis was a good halfway place to meet.

I had been planning for this get together for quite a while. Remembering my Scouting days with Jamie, I knew I had to keep the boys occupied. I acquired four bicycles and was ready to keep the boys busy come Monday morning. We got through Saturday night and Sunday by going to the La Salle swimming pool and the water slide out east of town.

We left Monday morning about 9:00 A.M. I had Lindy's old bicycle, and Jessie rode the three-speed I acquired from Floyd Esche. Mr. Zera dropped off the bike that Brett rode, and Evan rode the bike I picked up for $5.00 at a garage sale. I had the plastic milk carton and a ball of twine, all the equipment that was necessary for the start of the "great adventure."

Zooming down Bucklin Avenue and stopping just long enough at Third Street for the light to change, we proceeded down to the towpath via First and Marquette Streets. Jessie helped Brett and Evan get their bikes down the steps by Lock 14, and we were on our way to the viaduct over the Little Vermilion River. We rode our bikes down to the river and left them in tall grass.

I explained to the boys that I would go upstream and throw the empty milk carton into the river. When the milk carton floated by, they were to throw stones at it. I would pull the carton back up and repeat the process.

All went well for a couple of trips, but the boys got excited and decided they really wanted to sink that plastic milk carton. Evan got a huge rock, and while trying to get close to the moving object, got into the water. Wasn't long till all three were in the water having a ball. Well—what the heck. I walked out into the fast-flowing creek myself. It hadn't rained for a couple of weeks, so the river was really just a clean creek.

There was a logjam nearby the spot where the boys started throwing rocks, so I suggested that we break it up as an environmental project. They dug in and soon small limbs and big limbs were floating down the river. One limb was so big the boys could float on it, so I decided to let them ride it down to where the Vermilion empties into the Illinois River. Boy what fun that was!

When we got down to the Illinois River, I had some second thoughts about going any farther. I had them launch the log into the big Illinois River, and we all waved goodbye to our Tom Sawyer raft.

The Illinois River was low, so rather than retrace our steps I decided to let the boys walk in the river if they promised to keep near shore. All three are good swimmers and they didn't take any chances getting into deep water. Just to be on the safe side, however, I had them take off their shoes, which I carried. The river bottom turned from sand into mud, and that is when the mud fight began. They would reach into the river and come up with hands full of good clean silt that had settled on the bottom. Wasn't long till they were all black from head to toe.

We got out of the river where the new Abraham Lincoln Bridge crosses. A path there leads back up to the towpath. We washed as much mud off as we could, then I had the boys put their shoes back on for the walk to the bicycles.

We rode back through town by First and Marquette Streets, then up Bucklin. What a sight we must have been. Lindy couldn't believe what she saw. They stripped and got into the shower stalls immediately. After three tries, the clothing was finally clean enough to send home. Brett and Evan's underclothes were so dirty when they jumped into my shower stall, I had to get out the handheld vacuum cleaner to pick up the mud that fell on the floor.

Elders, Youngers Share Love of Music

From the *NewsTribune*, La Salle, Illinois, January 20, 1997:

Don Huling, who has played the violin since he was 9 and is a concert violinist, is more accustomed to playing to audiences than the rest of his band mates.

But that's all right with him. The other members of the Elders and Youngers band have more experience playing for dances than Huling does, so it sort of evens out.

"I'm the new guy on the block. I've been with them only since last November," he said.

The jazz band, which plays big band music from the '30s, '40s, and '50s, consists of members who are almost all senior

The Elders and Youngers Band

citizens, the oldest being 78. Then there are Marilyn and Ray Younger, who really are younger than the other members.

"Originally, we were called the Basement Band," said Harry Noel, 72, who plays cornet and flugelhorn. "We rehearsed in a basement then."

For a while, two women played in the band, and the six-piece act called themselves "Four Hits and Two Misses." When the Youngers joined, about two years ago, the act renamed itself the "Elders and Youngers."

The name was Ellworth (Danz)'s idea," Noel said. "We're older, but have the Youngers, who are also younger. But we'd probably keep the name if Marilyn and Ray quit."

The current lineup of the band is Marilyn Younger, tenor sax and clarinet; her husband Ray, the alto sax and clarinet; Aldo Piscia, rhythm guitar; Huling, mandolin and violin; Danz, alto sax and clarinet; and Noel, cornet and flugelhorn.

Noel was born in La Salle in 1924 and played in studio bands in California after World War II. "I was on the road a lot," he said. "I first played professionally when I was 13." He moved back to the Illinois Valley and played for such acts as the Johnny Kaye Band, Joe Dezutti, and Johnny Duffy.

"I played with all the name bands—the studio and road bands, all the local bands."

Huling came to popular music by way of a different route. Although he studied mechanical engineering at the University of Illinois, Urbana, he is also a concert violinist, playing since he was 9.

Which was not unusual in his family—they were all musically inclined. His mother and sister played the piano, and one brother played the cello and another played the flute.

"Dad didn't play anything. He listened mostly and encouraged the rest of us."

Huling stayed with music into his adolescence.

"I played in the La Salle-Peru high school orchestra. I was the first chair my junior and senior years, in 1940 and 1941."

He has also played with the Illinois Valley Symphony Orchestra and is on the board of the Illinois Valley Youth Symphony.

Huling's instrument, the mandolin, is traditionally a rhythm instrument. For the Elders and Youngers though, he puts it to a different use.

"I play it as a melody instrument. That's catching on now in dance bands," he said.

In spite of age differences (the Youngers are in their 50s) and a variety of backgrounds, the members of the band are drawn together by common love of music.

The Youngers, for instance, are the only two music majors in the band. They met while students at the University of Illinois, Urbana.

"Each of us has our own style and sense of humor," said

Marilyn Younger. "But the band is a good way to play with someone who improvises like Harry Noel."

The band practices about once each week, and though they do not have a heavy booking schedule they do get out and perform from time to time.

"Harry's not looking for a lot of places to play," Marilyn said. "Mostly, it's just what comes along."

These include nursing homes and the Rotary Club. Recently, they played in the Hotel Kaskaskia in La Salle. Their next gig will be on St. Patrick's Day at Care Inn Convalescent Center in La Salle.

"We'll keep going as long as we're all here," Noel said.

Our Junior College

Dr. E. Glenn Marshall was inducted into the IVCC-LPO (Illinois Valley Community College and La Salle–Peru–Oglesby Junior College) Hall of Fame Class of 2009 on Saturday, May 16, 2009. I was fortunate to be asked to accept my father-in-law's certificate. The recognition of Dr. Marshall's work and dedication to the school from its inception pleased our family and friends. What I took away from this prestigious occasion was what a fine junior college we have here in our community and what an opportunity young people have to obtain a great, affordable education.

Some of the other teachers mentioned by other members of the Class of 2009 were John Strell, football coach; Charles E. Korn, instructor in drafting and engineering; Katherine Reinhard, instructor in history and political science; and Earl Trobaugh, instructor in Latin, French, and English. Earl went on to become first President of IVCC.

I felt very comfortable sitting on the stage of the IVCC Cultural Centre with nine other men representing themselves or relatives of the honorees. When it came time for me to receive the award I was able to tell a short story concerning Dr. Marshall.

Glenn loved Indiana University. He had graduated from this school on October 14, 1933, with a PhD in Chemistry. He taught chemistry at the LPO Junior College from 1923 until he left this area in 1955 to continue teaching at Franklin College in Indiana, then returning to Illinois to teach at Eureka College. At age 94, Glenn's desire was to return to the college he loved most and do three things. He wanted to meet the president of the college, he wanted to meet the head of the chemistry department, and he wanted to meet Bobby Knight, who was head basketball coach at this time.

On June 18, 1981, we headed for Bloomington, Indiana. We got to talk with the assistant to the president, who greeted Glenn as one of the oldest alumni to return to the school. He contacted the local newspaper that took a picture of both of us that was shown on the large screen the night of the induction into the Hall of Fame. The head of the chemistry department was at Purdue, but Glenn got to read the paper he had prepared to Dr. Allerhand's secretary.

Our third and last goal was to meet Bobby Knight. We drove over to the Assembly Hall where Bobby had his office. He too was gone for the weekend, but Glenn received an autographed picture of Bobby we still have in our possession.

Hugh C. Price

Lindy's first piano teacher was Hugh C. Price, who also taught Virgil Fox and Zez Confrey. Lindy studied under Mr. Price's direction back in the 1930s. Their paths crossed a couple more times later in life.

As a teacher, Mr. Price concentrated on having his pupils play the right notes with the correct fingering at the tempo he wanted. He had Lindy study under the direction of Hubert Kaszynski, also one of Hugh Price's students. Hubert taught Lindy more of the feel or expression of the piece. Hubert went on to teach at Lamar University in Beaumont, Texas.

Lindy performed in a Twelve Piano Ensemble, under the direction of

Thurman and Agnes Huling, Starved Rock Lodge, 1945

Hugh Price, in Matthiessen Memorial Auditorium on Sunday, May 23, 1937. This event was sponsored by the Music Department of the La Salle Women's Club. Twelve Wurlitzer pianos were moved onto the stage. Listed on the program were 141 students in age groups six to ten, ten to fourteen, and high school students. Thirty-seven adults were featured in the opening and closing numbers. Also listed were the seventeen teachers of the students in the ensemble, from Peru, Oglesby, Ladd, Mendota, Spring Valley, and Tiskilwa, Illinois.

Five years later, Lindy taught at Sion Grade School while I was in Europe with the Ninth Army Air Force. The school was located out in the country one mile east of the Utica Four Corners and one mile north. She wanted to teach the children music, but the old piano was in such bad condition she couldn't use it. One of the first things she did that fall was to contact her former teacher, Hugh Price, and tell him about the piano. Hugh came out to the school, looked over the instrument, and told Lindy it could be fixed well enough for her to use it. He made a list of the strings that had to be replaced, the number of felts needed, and the number of "ivories" needed. She got permission from Mr. Ryan, head of the school board, to have Mr. Price buy the equipment. I think her selling point might have been when she told the frugal farmers that Mr. Price would do all the work free!

The piano was fixed when one day Mr. Spickerman, the school superintendent, visited her class. He was impressed with how enthused the students were with their singing. He told Lindy they would forget history dates but would enjoy music the rest of their lives.

Lindy's Sion Schoolchildren—1945

Charles Emerick	William Rogowski
Barbara Fitzgerald	Keith Ryan
David A. Rogowski	Anna Marie Thompson
Edmund Rogowski	George Thompson
Eileen Rogowski	John Dee Thompson
Mary Jo Rogowski	Nancy Thompson
Richard Rogowski	

Virgil Fox

Another famous pupil of Hugh C. Price was Virgil Fox. Virgil was born in Princeton, Illinois, May 3, 1912, and died in Palm Beach, Florida, October 25, 1980. He was an American organist known especially for his "heavy organ" concerts of the music of Bach. An article in the November 22, 1963, *NewsTribune,* La Salle, Illinois, stated "Fox is coming to the Tri-Cities Tuesday Nov. 26 to present the second concert of the season for the Tri-City Community Concert Association in the La Salle-Peru High School Matthiessen Auditorium." Fox performed on the school's unique Aeolian three-manual, forty-rank (2,500 pipes in all) organ.

Prior to this concert in La Salle, Virgil spent almost a week having the school's organ tuned and adjusted to his specifications. The pipes of this organ were usually behind heavy drapes, which muffled the tone from the organ. To overcome this problem Virgil had the drapes removed.

Mrs. Matthiessen donated the La Salle-Peru Township Aeolian Organ to the High School in 1929. I attended the Virgil Fox concert and remember sitting as close to the organ as possible. I wanted to watch Virgil's footwork when he played Bach's famous "Toccata and Fugue in D Minor." He played part of this number with just his feet, hitting four notes at a time. What a showman! What an organist! What an organ!

Watch Virgil Fox on the Internet at VirgilFoxLegacy. com. My favorite is Scott Joplin's rag "The Entertainer."

This L-P High School organ was rededicated on November 20, 1981. The original organ had been installed with a Duo-Art Player, with rolls similar to piano rolls. This mechanism was removed and replaced by a device that could have the organ play on "automatic." Mr. Evans, organist at the First Presbyterian Church of Chicago, came to the L-P High School on November 20, 1981, and performed on the rebuilt organ, which was lifted from the auditorium floor and placed on the stage. Mr. Evans had a very attractive young lady stand next to him and turn the sheet music pages for him. We in the audience were surprised and pleased when Mr. Evans got up from the organ bench while the organ continued to play a famous waltz and danced on stage with his beautiful page-turner. He had put the organ on the automatic mode.

This information was obtained from Pam Lange, Director of the Bureau County Historical Society and Museum. I had contacted numerous organists and people who were at the concert but couldn't confirm the date. I contacted Wanda Lent, organist at the La Salle Congregational Church, and Ruth Moyle, organist at the Oglesby Union Church. They both mentioned his red cape and great showmanship.

Despite (or perhaps because of) his controversial approach to organ music, Virgil Fox attained a celebrity status not unlike that of Leonard Bernstein and Glenn Gould. The *New York Times* said of him, twenty years after his death, "Fox could play the pipe organ like nobody's business, but that is not all that made him unforgettable to so many people across the country. He made classical organ music appeal even to audiences that normally wouldn't be expected to sit still for it."

Veterans History Project

From the *NewsTribune*, La Salle, Illinois, May 23, 2006:

Rotarians hear about veterans history project

The U.S. Library of Congress's "Veterans History Project" was the program topic at last week's meeting of La Salle Rotary. It was presented by Rotarian Don Huling, who noted that the project is intended to help preserve our nation's history. Authorized by Congress, it's an effort to collect stories and experiences of the nation's war veterans and those who supported them at home. Huling already has submitted his own experiences as a World War II radio operator in Europe.

"The nearest official site for persons volunteering to participate in the project is in DeKalb, Ill.," he said. Information is available on the Internet at www.loc.gov/folklife/vets/.

One of Huling's wartime experiences was a trip to Paris, France, to see the Glen Miller Orchestra at the Grand Hotel. Miller had enlisted in the war effort, along with his entire band, to provide morale building music for the troops. Not only was Huling able to see the performance in the famed Mirror Room, a surprise visitor at the concert was Gen. Dwight D. "Ike" Eisenhower, Supreme Allied Commander.

Friendship

April 22, 2007

TV is so bad after we watch Wheel of Fortune that I have been getting old movies from the Peru Library to watch in the evening. Last night we watched an oldie entitled *Du Berry Was a Lady* that starred Red Skelton and Lucile Ball. The plot is rather thin, but the highlights for me included really good swing music by the Tommy Dorsey Orchestra and the final number by the entire cast entitled "Friendship."

The movie is based on the 1939 Broadway production of *Du Berry Was a Lady,* starring Ethel Merman and Bert Lahr. Cole Porter wrote the music for the entire show. The final number, "Friendship," became Bert Lahr's signature song. When it was performed in New Haven, Connecticut, before going to New York, the audience liked it so much that Porter jumped up from the second row in the audience and introduced another verse.

When I was in basic training way back in 1943 down in Sheppard Field, Texas, a couple of buddies of mine and I sang this song so many times we got the rest of the GIs mad at us. Here is how this came about:

The two buddies had attended one year at the University of Illinois before being drafted into the Army, as I had been. They both had been involved with ROTC. U of I is a land-grant school, and therefore the men were required to participate in ROTC, which consists of, among other things, close-order drill. I had had a fair amount of this kind of disciplinary activity in the Boy Scouts. So when it came time for all of us new GIs to go on our required twenty-mile hike, which was part of our basic training, the three of us were in pretty good shape.

Now about the song "Friendship." All three of us were familiar with it, as it had become popular in the 1943 movie we had all seen recently at the post exchange movie house. The three of us got together at the rear of the long column as we marched out of camp and headed north toward Oklahoma. This was great fun for me. I had hiked twenty miles or more from Ottawa to Utica and back in order to get a Boy Scout award. I felt like singing, and what better song to sing than "Friendship." The other two fellows joined in, and we had a ball, even though we drove the rest of the fellows nuts. They were grumbling about the hike, and we were singing! When they started to gripe out loud, we just fell further and further back and kept singing.

Cyclops
by Jamie Huling

I'm not sure I knew I was setting out on an important journey when I announced that I wanted a car for my sixteenth birthday. My idea had been a modest little sports car tied up with a bow. My father's idea was to get me a job with Cyclops Welding so I could save up and buy one for myself.

Cyclops Welding and Manufacturing was owned and operated by the Piano brothers, three second-generation Italians. It was located just south of First Street in a dark, sooty building a few blocks up from the old Illinois and Michigan Canal. Joe Piano stayed in the shop, running the day-to-day business and metal fabrication while his two brothers, Tony and Frank, headed out into the surrounding county in trucks loaded down with bottles of gas clanking against arc welders, fabricated steel, and whatever tools were needed for the job that day. They had learned their trade in the shipyards of World War II and belonged to the Boilermakers Union. None of them had all their fingers. I was terrified.

I showed up for work the first day wearing cut-off shorts and tennis shoes in a shop that was lit up like the Fourth of

July from hot sparks flying everywhere. After getting all the trucks out the door and off to their various destinations, Joe turned his weathered face with the ever present Kool nonfilter in the corner of his mouth to give me an ill-concealed, fairly disgusted once over.

"Jamesy. You're going to catch fire dressed up like that. You be sure and show up with coveralls and steel-toed boots tomorrow. Ya hear?"

My name is Jamie but I don't think Joe could bring himself to call me such a girly sounding name. Without protective clothing, I was given the job of cleaning the toilet for the first time in its twenty-year existence and removing enormous, rusted nuts from even larger, rusted bolts the rest of the day. My high-school buddies were impressed that I was working for the Boilermakers. I hadn't thought too much about the macho image of my summer job until then, and I immediately traded in my small-town, Midwest, surfer-boy shuffle for a more manly swagger and started paying attention to what the Piano brothers might teach me.

The Pianos were gruff, no-nonsense men who did jobs that would get you dismembered or killed if you got silly. When they said the word "Work" you could hear the capital W in their voices, and they'd been as much a part of winning WWII as any GI. Frank told me that if there was too big of a gap between the plate steel on a ship, he wouldn't stop. He'd just yell for bigger welding rods and more heat. I got my first case of burnt eyes watching him weld up a dredging bucket next to the Illinois River. Nobody had warned me about the reflection from the water. Tony talked me across the first scaffolding board I froze up on. He yelled up at me to sit down and skootch across when I turned into a Greek statue, twenty feet above a hissing, thundering collection of gargantuan pressure cookers. I was debating how much attention I should be paying to a guy who'd already broken his back twice falling off of scaffolds, when he threatened to come up and carry me across. That finally got me moving.

I spent more time in the shop with Joe than out in the field, so it was Joe who had the most influence on me. Even though I was just the twerp, son of an engineer, I could sense that Joe was pleased when I told him I wanted to learn how to cut and weld. He wouldn't let me use good welding rods but allowed me to pick up the little rod butts at the end of the day and go out back and practice on scrap. He showed me how to cut enormous sheets of steel on a shear without losing a finger and how to hold a disc grinder so I wouldn't lose precious work time at the emergency room getting stitched up.

After a few weeks I got up the courage to walk with the rest of the crew up to the bank on payday. We'd line up behind the guys in suits and ties, and it was a proud thing to be calloused and dirty from working hard all day. This was nineteen-sixties, industrial America, and we Boilermakers were keeping it running. The only compliment I got from Joe that summer was for putting a muffler on the big flatbed truck. Though happy as a puppy who'd just learned to pee on the newspaper, I was kind of hoping he'd actually let me weld something, but metal and welding rods were too expensive to let a helper fool with.

I remained mildly terrified of the Piano brothers and the job that entire summer, but in the fall I bought a used car and a little motorcycle. My father had taught me the importance of working for something I wanted, and Joe, Frank, and Tony Piano had taught me to be proud of being a worker. I ended up becoming a carpenter and scaring the crap out of my own helpers over the years. Yelling at them to get their faces in their work because "you can't see what you're doing with your eyes closed and your head turned away." If I was feeling particularly "Pianoesque," I'd follow it with, "The only thing worse than a sissy is two sissies."

I understood I had finally come home one weekend on a Habitat for Humanity build when a doctor friend of mine froze in terror up on the roof. I hollered up at him to just sit down and skootch across, which he did. When he got to the ladder and had the top rung in a death grip with one of his million-dollar hands, he raised the other one and gave me a thumbs up. The universal sign for Work with a capital W.

PART IV

POST-WAR STORIES BY PAUL HULING

Patience + Perseverance = Happiness

When I was eighteen, I was not ready for college. I was in the U.S. Navy. When I was nineteen the war ended, but I was still not ready for college. The fact is, I had never seriously considered my future education; I had only thought far enough ahead to serve my country and get my discharge. Life after the Navy was an unknown. I had no idea what a future would be like without a depression or war.

I had had enough gumption to take college preparatory subjects in high school even though the prospects of my attaining a higher education seemed remote to me. Also, I had not enlisted until I had enough credits to graduate, a fortunate move.

When I was discharged in July, 1946, it was already too late to enroll in the school of my choice, General Motors Institute, but I tried anyway. The school advised me, in my rejection, to attend college and pick up more math before applying again.

So I did as I was advised and was later accepted. The extra effort and patience were well worth it. I was ready now.

Before entering GMI, I had been dating a most wonderful girl named Jean. The day came when she went away to Wellesley, Massachusetts, for four years and I headed for Flint, Michigan, to GMI. Somehow those years increased our bond. We made it!

As I think about the delays that were placed in my "road of life," I think about how much they added strength. Many times when things don't go my way, right away, I may think I've lost out and will never have the opportunity to attain them. But patience, plus perseverance, adds up to happiness. I know.

"His Eye Is on the Sparrow . . ."

It was a beautiful autumn Sunday afternoon as I was driving through Bucks County, Pennsylvania. The year was 1946. I had just recently been discharged from the Navy. Not many cars traveled the back roads of Bucks County, because most cars were in pretty bad shape and tires were not yet plentiful enough for most cars to have replaced their worn-out treads.

One beautiful scene in a wide valley was a farm, probably Quaker, surrounded by many trees in full color. The farm was bordered by the road. In fact, the road hugged two sides of the bright red barn, making a very tight curve.

As we approached the barn I stopped the car. There was no stop sign, I just stopped. "Why did I do that?" I asked myself. There was plenty of width for me to make the turn and stay on my side of the road.

Then the answer: a motorcycle zoomed past the hood of the car and went into the ditch, totally missing the turn. Another motorcycle skidded past, barely staying on the road but using both lanes of the sharp curve. A third bike screeched and slid right up to the side of the car.

The rider said, "We were racing. Never saw you on the turn. Thanks for stopping."

The Shake-Down Road Test

June, 1947. When my brother John graduated from Iowa State in Ames, Iowa, the only person in my family who could attend the graduation ceremony was me . . . that is, if I could make it that far in "Bessie," the name I gave my first car, a recently acquired 1931 Model A Ford, two-door sedan.

A friend of mine called Johnny volunteered to go with me.

The trip was to be the shake-down road test for my very used Model A. The plan was to pick up brother John from Ames (about 300 miles), drive back to La Salle, Illinois (another 300 miles), drive brother John to Hyde Park, New York (about 800 miles), then drive myself to Easton, Pennsylvania (another 100 miles), to seek summer employment, ending with the return trip to La Salle, Illinois (about 800 miles), to start my next term in junior college.

My friend Johnny and I left La Salle one very hot day at about noon. Nine hours later, we had traveled about forty miles. We had been twelve miles short of Dixon, Illinois, when the wind picked up and blew so hard against the windshield that the outside visor, along with the overhead oak beam, which was quite rotten, lifted up about an inch on the driver's side. This blew in a huge amount of dust and rotten wood, and required the driver to reach up and hold down the roof of the car, lest it blow off completely.

This first incident was quickly followed by a second, which was that one of the two blades of the fan broke off, causing the remaining blade to be so out of balance it broke the water pump in half. Of course, this caused all the water to run out of the cooling system rather quickly, so we pulled off the road as the wind raged on.

We parked in a farmer's barnyard. No one was home. We then hitchhiked to Dixon to pick up a water pump, fan, and a bracket to hold the roof on. The '36 Chevy that gave us a ride was also having problems. Something in the steering had broken, which required the driver to turn the steering wheel one full revolution before any change in direction would take place. It was difficult to drive into a fierce headwind when it required one full turn to make a minor correction.

The ride back to the farmyard was in a car that seemed to have no flaws. Luckily I had my Navy flashlight, because it was dark before we got under way again. We drove on, thinking we would drive all night to make up for lost time.

About midnight we pulled into a gas station, but it was closed for the night. We drove on to a few more and they were all closed. Because we were tired, we decided to sleep until one station opened. But as the wind blew, the car rocked and the temperature dropped. We were too cold to sleep, and neither of us had brought sweaters.

As it began to rain, and we were cold, we decided we'd drive on looking for gas rather than sit and freeze. We lucked out; we found a gas station that opened early. The gas gauge had been on empty a long time. Now we were really ready to make time, we thought.

But increasingly heavy rainfall slowed us down. Old US Route 30 in Iowa had been built with raised edges, which tended to keep water on the highway rather than let it run off. In low places the water pooled, making it slow going. Many cars had hydroplaned off the road but didn't want our help.

As the morning progressed, the farm fields began to overflow onto the highway. The water got to be so deep in places that whoever was in the passenger seat would have to push down extra hard on the floorboards with his feet, so the force of the water beneath them would not cause the boards to float and interfere with the driver's feet.

We passed a billboard on which was a picture of a man swimming. The water level of the flooded field made it look like the man in the picture was swimming in the field. A picture of what we saw appeared in *Life* magazine the following week.

We finally made it through to Ames. We were very wet and very tired. We were greeted by my surprised brother John, who had called the State Police and had been told there were so many cars abandoned on US 30, nobody was making it through to Ames.

Two days later, after graduation, we headed back to Illinois with the damp back seat of the Model A full of everything brother John owned. At first the car didn't start. Dead. After a push, it seemed okay. We drove a few blocks and stopped for breakfast. Dead again when we went to start it. Another push, and brother John drove as the car backfired and carried on. For some reason John turned on the headlights, and the car was fine, that is, until the bulbs burned out. Then he honked the klaxon horn. As long as the ah-*ooga* horn was blowing, the car ran fine! When he stopped the horn, the car would also stop running smoothly and backfire.

I discovered the problem was under the floorboards. The force of the water pressure under the floor had literally lifted the ground cable off the battery post. The only ground for the generator was through the horn, but one had to honk it to keep current flowing.

That problem solved, brother John drove on a few miles and announced he was having trouble keeping the car headed straight. Next he shouted that there was a tire alongside of the car, going the same speed we were. It was ours! It was our wheel!

This time it was a broken front spring. Every leaf except the main leaf had broken and fallen out along the highway as we drove. This allowed the front wheels and the axle between them to drift from one side to the other.

We stopped at a hardware store and bought a stack of flat washers to make up the space where the leaves had been before they fell out.

Now it was noon and we had traveled about 30 miles. Everything went fine until darkness came; then I had to buy new headlight bulbs, parking light bulbs, and tail and stoplight bulbs in order to drive on to La Salle.

Brother John took the bus to Hyde Park, New York. I worked on the Model A a week before I took off for Easton,

Pennsylvania, without any problems. I returned to La Salle by way of upstate New York, adding water every half hour because the fan I bought in Dixon, that first trip, flew off and went right through the radiator. I fixed the hole in the radiator with a bar of Fels-Naptha soap, good enough to make the trip, except adding water as I went.

Over the next three years, I drove that Model A hard and fast for 60,000 miles. About the only thing I didn't take apart in that time was the doors from the hinges. From a previous owner, I learned the car had 180,000 miles on it before I bought it. I sold it for ten dollars less than I paid for it.

A Christmas Tree Christmas

"I'm looking for a three- or four-foot Christmas tree," I said to Joe. "Do you have any left?"

"Are you kidding?" Joe responded. "I haven't had a small one for a week! People have to buy the big ones and cut them off. . . . 'Course, I still charge by the size, 'cause most people don't cut them down in size once they get 'em home. Why are you looking for one, anyway?"

That was a good question. I didn't need one. I was boarding, attending college, and working part-time for a Pontiac dealer. It was the Parts Manager, Frank, who asked me to try and locate a tree, and I had told him I thought I could find one at my friend Joe's gas station during my lunch hour.

The problem was that it was 1947, the second Christmas after WWII, and nearly everyone wanted a Christmas tree! Those who had sold trees during the war had no idea how great the demand would be that Christmas. Besides, during the war Christmas trees were not a high priority item, so tree farmers had not been able to take good care of their stock. Most of the trees for sale that year looked like the tree we'd see on TV a few years later in "Charlie Brown's Christmas."

Frank had told me his father was having a tough time with depression this Christmas season. Frank's mom had died that year, and Frank was living with his father, just the two of them, in a big house that had served as the family gathering place each Christmas. Even his brother, who had three small children, wasn't planning to come home for Christmas. Christmas for Frank and his dad was going to be an exchange of socks and ties as they listened to the radio. So Frank thought that maybe if he brought home a small tree, he and his dad could reminisce as they decorated it.

As I looked at the very, very picked-over trees in Joe's lot, I shook my head at the sorry state of affairs. The only tree that looked good was the one he had standing out near the street to attract customers. And it was twelve feet tall! Also, priced at twelve dollars! A dollar a foot?

"Who'll buy that one?" I asked Joe. "The top looks good," I added, to imply I really would cut it off.

"You want it?" said Joe. "You can have it, stand and all, for a buck and a half!"

"How come?" I asked.

"'Cause it's Christmas Eve and I want to close up," replied Joe.

"Deal," I said.

You should have seen the look on Frank's face when I pulled up in front of the dealership with a twelve-foot Christmas tree tied to the top of my Model A Ford!

"I'll deliver it to your house," I said, "and you owe me a buck and a half!"

I thought Frank looked like Santa Claus as he laughed. As I drove off, Frank just shook his head.

Christmas morning I got a phone call. It was Frank. He was very happy. Here's why. . . .

After work on Christmas Eve, Frank went home and found his dad in the living room surrounded by all the lights and ornaments they had ever collected over the years. No way was he going to let Frank cut the bottom off that tree, when the ceilings in their old Victorian house were twelve feet high. He had moved all the furniture to make room for the tree, and they were "going to do it right, by golly."

As they decorated, Frank's dad became happier by the minute. Life wasn't so bad after all. Then the phone rang; it was Frank's brother. He had managed to get some time off. They would be there within two hours with their kids!

Frank and his father frantically searched the stores, still open 'til nine that Christmas Eve, and bought presents enough to fill the car. It was going to be Christmas after all, a Merry Christmas!

"That buck and a half tree made three little kids and four adults very happy," said Frank proudly.

It made my day, too.

The Famous Squad Car

The year was 1949. I had been working for the local Pontiac dealer just a short time when I noticed the old squad car in the storage area. All the emblems were removed, but I knew at first glance it was the old police car. I didn't give it much thought for weeks after first seeing it. Then one day Les, the car salesman, began rummaging around the storage area looking for something to clean up and put up for sale. He looked like he could use some help moving cars about, so I asked him if I could be of any use. He was happy to have the offer, so he moved the first and I the second and so on till we reached the Studebaker that wouldn't start.

I commented, "Might know the old squad car wouldn't start."

"What? What did you say? What do you mean squad car?" asked Les. "Who told you that was a squad car?"

"Nobody told me," I said. "But that's the old squad car."

"How do you know? What makes you think so?" asked Les again.

"I don't know how I know. No other car looks quite like it. I could tell it a mile away. Maybe it's the way it sits, or the red wheels. That car has personality, a reputation, character. It's as easy to spot as a person," I said.

"Yeah, that's it," he said. "I've had it in storage six months in hopes it would be forgotten; then you spot it right off. Do me a favor and just don't refer to this car as the 'old police car,' okay?"

So the old Studebaker was shined up for resale. The idea was to sell it as a normal used car, not a used police car. When I next saw it, the wheels were green, and Les asked me if that helped camouflage it. It really didn't, but I allowed him to think it did.

Les sold the Studebaker a few days later to a young man from a small town about twenty miles away.

About a month later, here came the Studebaker and the new owner to see Les.

"Was this car a police car before I bought it?" he asked. Les tried to hedge a bit on the answer.

"Well, it was, and you know it! I just might sue you!" said the man.

Les quickly replied, "Maybe we can work something out."

I don't know all the details of what was worked out, but when the old squad car entered the shop to be worked on, I was friendly with the owner. He was very calm and had no animosity toward the dealer or the salesman. I asked him how he knew the car had been a police car, and he told me his friend had followed him one night on a dusty road just after he had washed the car. When the headlights hit the back of the Studebaker just right, he could read POLICE on the trunk lid.

Other than that he liked the big heavy car. So we ground off all the paint and had it repainted. Even so, he paid us a visit about six months later and said he was approached about once a month by strangers who asked him if that wasn't the old squad car.

He felt his car was famous!

Flying with Dennis

I had not planned to fly back to Michigan from New York, but driving east for a long weekend from school, we had hit a deer and could not drive the car back to school. The year was 1949.

Neither Dennis (my classmate who had also been in the car which hit the deer) nor I had ever flown commercial airlines. We arrived at La Guardia airport early to buy tickets. Dennis took over. The ticket windows formed a circle around the customer area. Dennis stood in the center of the circle (hardly any other people were there at the time) and loudly broadcast that he needed four tickets to Detroit, NOW, and which airline could give him the best deal. Dennis was from Brooklyn and this was New York; the ticket agents understood very well there would be no peace within the ticket area until they removed this loud nuisance. We got a good deal from American Airlines. I can't remember much about my first flight except buying the tickets and what happened after that at the terminal.

As we waited for our flight, the airport began to fill up with more travelers. Soon a crowd of people began gathering in the lounge area. I went in to see what was going on. There sat Eleanor Roosevelt, alone. People had formed a circle about twenty feet in diameter around her, as though there was a fence or line which they could not cross. She was trying to read; however, it was apparent she was uncomfortable with all these people surrounding her, just staring.

I was about to slip away when in walked Dennis. He looked the situation over and without hesitation walked up to Mrs. Roosevelt, extended his hand, said something to her, to which she responded, then sat down beside her engaged in happy conversation. The crowd of people dissolved almost immediately.

Eleanor Roosevelt

It wasn't very long before Mrs. Roosevelt left to catch her flight. What on earth was going on with Dennis?

"I didn't know you knew her!" I said.

"Well, I didn't," said Dennis, "but I knew the people would leave her alone as soon as she met her 'companion.' So I asked her if she wanted a companion until the crowd dispersed. She thanked me and asked me to please sit down. Nice lady; we had a little chat."

I learned that even famous people sometimes need help from strangers.

Lake-Effect Snow

It started out as a warm winter day in February. 1950. My classmate, Don, and I were driving home to Illinois from Flint, Michigan, when the weather began to change rather suddenly. First there was some wind, then gusts that grew colder the farther south we went. We weren't worried about the weather inside my Pontiac because it had a nice heater.

Then, there sounded a sudden explosion which came from the engine compartment. The car vibrated and shook violently, almost leaving the road because the vibration made it hard to hold the steering wheel. There was also a terrible knocking sound.

One look under the hood told us the problem: an engine connecting rod had broken and exited the engine by way of a large hole it had created as it left the engine block. Everything under the hood was covered with oil.

So we sat off Route 27 and contemplated our next move as the wind grew colder and icy snow began to fall. Here we were, north of Angola, Indiana, soon to become involved in what I have since learned is called an Alberta Clipper snow-belt lake-effect snowstorm. A bad one.

There was another student attending the same school (General Motors Institute, now Kettering University), who would be leaving school two hours after we left and driving to Illinois. We could wait for him, as he would know my car. That seemed like a better idea than hitching a ride and abandoning my car with all our belongings. So we sat about twenty minutes before we realized the storm was growing much worse than we expected, and we were freezing cold. Also, the car was no longer distinguishable as mine because ice and snow had just about blotted out its make and model.

We figured it was about twelve miles to Angola. If I could start the engine on seven cylinders, how long would it run before it bound up completely? Could we control the car? Where might we stall out? Hopefully, closer to town was better than sitting where we were. And we'd have heat.

Amazingly, the engine started. It made an awful racket, like a cement mixer full of hammers. I soon learned there was one rpm where there was the least amount of roughness; I would try to drive the car at that rpm. That rpm, we soon found, was equal to 36 miles per hour. Any less than 36 mph the car would sort of gyrate, and at speeds over 36 mph the vibration would get so bad the windows would roll down and the radio would change stations. So we drove 36 mph, allowing what little traffic was now on the road to pass.

The radiator did not boil. This was real good news; it meant the water jacket of the engine had not cracked, which would have allowed the antifreeze coolant to leak out.

About six miles from Angola the engine started another round of hammering and banging. As I looked for a place to pull off the road, the noise quit as suddenly as it started, so I just drove on. We made it to the first gas station since the engine blew the rod. We were in Angola.

A good look at the engine through the now larger hole revealed half of the connecting rod was wrapped around the crankshaft and the other half had been thrown out. We didn't know where the piston was.

The man at the station told us the nearest Pontiac dealer was eight miles east. We wanted to go west, where the nearest Pontiac dealer was twenty miles. Knowing the friend who might spot us would never go east we decided to head twenty miles west. There was no oil in the engine, because it had splashed out, so we added five quarts and took off with five more quarts in the back seat. The oil gauge now read just a little more than zero. That was good news, too. But the weather was bad news.

So we drove about ten miles west before the oil gauge read zero and we dumped the five more quarts of oil into the large hole in the side of the engine. By the time we got to LaGrange, the twenty miles, the oil pressure was back to zero, the storm was picking up speed, and more icy snow was drifting on the highway. In fact, no one had passed us since we left Angola because we were keeping up with traffic at 36 mph. Trucks were now pulling off the road to wait out the storm.

The Pontiac dealer was not very sympathetic to my problem. It would take about a week to obtain an engine and work me into his schedule. While I was talking my companion, Don, was in the service department borrowing some tin snips and fashioning an old one-gallon metal can to the size and shape of the hole in the engine. This would greatly reduce the amount of oil thrown out. He also filled four one-gallon cans with drain oil, oil already used by someone else, and placed them in the car. The oil was free. We were ready to head west again, next big town Elkhart, twenty-two miles. No letup in the storm.

By the time we reached Elkhart, we were passing whatever was traveling at less than 36 mph and no one was passing us. At one point we had to stop to clear ice off the windshield because it had piled up so high at the end of the wiper stroke that the blades quit moving. Then it was back to the road for a few miles before we would have to either add oil or clean the windshield. The snow left two tracks behind us now. There were no tracks in front; we were the only ones left on US 20 all across Indiana.

Once we got to Illinois, things were different. Instead of lake-effect snow, Illinois had had freezing rain. Glare ice on the roads; wires hanging with high voltage arcing to ground; icy tree limbs on the roads, on parked cars, on houses—while we cruised along at 36 mph doing our things.

My classmate's father was a Buick dealer, so Don gave me directions. The dealership was in St. Charles. We very nearly lost it on the turn to go south; luckily no one was in the intersection, because we used all the lanes available spinning the car round and round to head south after it had gone west for so long. It was now raining and freezing as it hit. There were no salt trucks.

When we arrived at the Buick dealership, Don opened the doors so I could drive in and melt some of the ice before I headed out on the last eighty miles alone, and at night. But the car couldn't make it up the sloping ramp to the door; there was so much ice and frozen snow packed under the fenders and hanging from the frame that the car was hung up on the ramp from the street to the sidewalk. It took a wrecker cable to hoist and pull the car into the garage. With the ice off the car, I was pretty sure I could make it home.

I did make it home to La Salle very late that night, after driving the broken car 300 miles and using 40 quarts of oil. It had been a long, tiring day.

Monday morning I went to work at the Pontiac dealership, which was my sponsor for GMI. As I walked in I stopped and talked with the service manager and told him I thought my Pontiac might need a tune-up if he had time that day, but tomorrow would be okay, too . . . no hurry, I told him.

You should have heard the noise when Bud, the mechanic, drove my car into the shop. He put the pedal to the metal and let the engine rev-up till it exploded and died. I was home.

By the way, the classmate who would follow us home two hours later never made it that day. He got stuck in the snow before he reached Angola.

Who's in Control?

Do I have a guardian angel? I think so!

Early one fall morning in 1950 I began a drive from Pennsylvania to Boston to see my sweetheart, Jean. This was before interstate highways, so most of the driving was mountainous. Breezing down a long straight hill, I gained speed to make it easily up the next incline. There was a slow-moving state highway truck up ahead which would be no problem to pass—no problem, that is until I was already in the left lane, passing. At that moment the state truck began a left turn to go into the woods on the left side of the road. I couldn't stop, too late. I couldn't pass on the right, too late. If I hit the ditch I would hit the culvert the truck was about to cross over. The shoulder of the road was just half a car width wide. I took the shoulder and felt the car slipping into the ditch as the truck continued to occupy more and more of the left lane.

What happened next was the rear of my car slid farther into the ditch while the front wheels maintained one wheel on the shoulder and the other on the edge of the ditch. The rear of the car began to slide more. I would have slammed into the culvert sideways except the embankment to the culvert served as a ramp, throwing the car high into the air. There was no space between the car and the front end of the truck, yet I did not touch the truck.

As the car was projected upward, I was thrown out of the driver's seat. (No seat belts back then.) While in the air I clung to the steering wheel with my left hand to keep from falling against the passenger side door. The car came down on the right shoulder of the road. Once again the rear end slid into the ditch while the front end managed to hang, one wheel on the road and one wheel on the shoulder. The impact of hitting the ground caused the suitcase in the back seat of the car to be thrown into the front seat between me and the steering wheel I was still clinging to. The car was now back on the road sliding sideways to the left. I grabbed the top of the steering wheel with my right hand. The car began to straighten out. The suitcase still prevented me from applying the brakes. I had over-corrected.

So the car went into another spin to the right. A couple more times I over-corrected trying to straighten out the car. All this swaying threw the suitcase to the front floor and enabled me to slide behind the steering wheel again, gaining full control of steering, but not braking. Finally, I was able to move the suitcase out of the way of my feet. The car was still moving in the correct direction, at a much reduced speed. I did not stop. The car and I both shook as I drove on.

It was about five miles later that I finally pulled the car into the first gas station I came to for inspection. The right rear tire was going flat. Grass and dirt were wedged between the tire and the wheel. Removing the tire and inspecting it, I saw the tire sidewall was cracked and had pinched the inner tube, causing the air leak. A check of the left rear wheel found more dirt and grass that looked like it was growing from between the tire and the rim. That tire was also cracked. During the next couple hundred miles, both front tires went flat from similar damage.

I remember my knees shaking as I stopped the car at that gas station. I don't remember thanking the Lord for my safety. Later on that day, as I greeted Jean, I do remember thanking God. And I've thanked Him over and over again for driving my car that day, because it was certainly not under my control.

Do I have a guardian angel? I think so!

The '37 Ford 60

"Les, what's wrong?" I asked, as Les stood on the customer side of the parts department counter at Inter City Motor Sales, a Pontiac dealer back about 1950. I knew something was troubling Les because he had a piece of paper in his hand and his head down like what it said was more troubling than he could bear.

"It's that '37 Ford 60 I took in on trade; I allowed too much for it," said Les sadly. Les was the car salesman.

"I told you not to go for that lemon," I needled Les. When I had seen it driven up in front of the dealership, with the owner talking to Les, I had clued Les in first chance I had. I knew that car. I knew that owner. He had bought the car about a year before and had driven hell out of it by hot-rodding around town. It only had 60 horsepower even though it was a V-8. My '31 Model A Ford could outrun that '37 Ford 60 around town, especially on the hills, but on the straightaway the Ford 60 could cruise along at 70 mph quite well.

The kid who owned the Ford 60 had spent a lot of money fixing it up, which was typical of the times. New cars were scarce and expensive, not much negotiating room for a deal because the dealers had the advantage. Sort of a "take it or leave it" attitude from the salesmen. The cars traded in had been though the war, that is, WWII, because no cars were made for civilian use during the war. The salesmen wanted clean '40, '41, and '42 cars to be traded in because they had generally been carefully nurtured through the war years. There was a pride in owning a '40, '41, or '42 car in 1950 because it was "almost" new.

Once a car was taken in trade, the dealer would go over it and restore it with new paint or polish, seat covers, and mechanical work. A clean '40, '41, or '42 would sell for more than its original value and half or more of what a new car cost. The trade-in for a '40, '41, or '42 would generally be a more-used '35, '36, or '37, which might be cleaned up a little, but not much, then sold. The trade-in would be just about worn out in most cases, generally worth $30 junk or $100, "as-is off the lot."

Well, Les had allowed too much for the '37 Ford 60. He saw all the glitz: the seat covers, new bright blue paint, red wheels, and chrome hub caps. He didn't drive it up one of the hills in town until after he had made the trade. He said the car smoked so bad he had to roll down the windows when he came to a hill.

"Otherwise, it's not bad," said Les.

"How's the oil pressure?" I asked. The first thing one looked for was oil pressure when checking out a V-8 Ford back then. If the pressure gauge went halfway at start-up and dropped off to one-fourth after warm-up, the engine was pretty good; if it didn't drop much at all after warm-up, the engine was better. This Ford barely made it to one-quarter at start-up, then dropped to zero. Les had a problem, and I knew it.

"What will it take for me to get $500 for this car?" he asked.

"Start with a new engine," I said. ("New" meant a rebuilt engine.) "At a cost of about $150," I added.

"I can't do that!" said Les, "I'd lose money!" To lose money on a car trade was a sin unless it was the last car in the trade sequence where a $50 car wouldn't sell and would have to go to junk for $30.

"Okay, Les, I'll put it to you straight. I can fix that car so you can sell it—for under $10—if you don't ask me any questions."

"How are you going to fix it?" he had to ask.

"I said, 'Don't ask.' And don't sell it to a friend, and don't guarantee it won't use oil," I responded.

Les grabbed his wallet and took out $10 which he thrust at me joyfully. "Here, I won't ask!"

"Wait, wait! That's your money, put it away. I'll bill the used car account. Now don't sell it before I fix it; my plan may not work as well as I hope. Just don't ask, and don't tell anybody I had anything to do with it."

Les was so happy he danced back to his desk.

I took off, in the Ford 60, to the local Western Tire and Auto parts store. I had my toolbox in the back seat. I parked behind the store. I bought a new oil filler cap . . . this one was special; it had a very long flexible hose as part of the assembly. I installed it in such a way that the long flexible hose wrapped around the back of the small engine, and I securely stuffed the open end of it into the carburetor air cleaner. When you stood on the oil filler side of the engine, the flex hose disappeared below the engine and the open end was not visible. If you stood on the other side of the engine, it looked like a special flex hose was part of the air cleaner. Now all the oil smoke from the engine was sucked into the carburetor instead of billowing into the car. (I might mention here that all new cars are now required to do an adaptation of this to reduce pollution.)

The other item I bought was a small vial of "new car scent." It looked like a fountain pen and once opened gave off a smell that was supposed to smell like a new car. It didn't help make the car smell new, but it masked some of the oily smell, or mixed with it, and one had the impression the car didn't actually stink. Later on I did take a soapy rag to wash off the entire interior of the car, which was covered with burnt oil scum. I hid the open vial under the dash.

One last fix: I removed the oil gauge. Naturally it read zero, so I bent the needle until it said one-quarter and replaced it. (Who looks at gauges when the engine is off? Do you look to see if the oil light is lit before you start your car?) I assumed no one would look at the gauge before starting the engine.

Returning the car to Les, I had second thoughts about what I had just done. I had been clever. I had acted like a typical non-reputable car salesman. I had thought I would never do business like that. But I had. I swore I would never do anything like that again and I haven't. Almost fifty years later it still bothers me. When I left the auto business, the last dealer I worked for told me I probably wouldn't have made a very good dealer because I was too honest. He may have been right. But he didn't last long, either.

Les drove the car home for lunch. He drove it home that night. He drove that car over the weekend. He loved it! He said, "Leave it in second gear and you can go 50! Keep it in low and you can whiz right up the hills!"

"Have you checked the oil, Les?" I asked.

"No, why?" was his reply.

"Better do that," was all I said.

Later: "Add a couple quarts of cheap oil to the used car account, will you, Paul?" That was Les.

One day Les came up to the parts department counter and said, "Well, I sold the Ford 60!"

"What did you take in on trade?" was all I could say.

"No trade. An out and out sale. Cash deal. Made out great!" said Les.

I was worried. I worried that one day that Ford 60 would be out in front of the dealership with an irate customer cussing me out demanding his money back. This worry went on for weeks. Then one day it did drive up in front. The owner got out and walked toward the front door. I left the parts department counter and went out into the shop in back, sort of hiding.

Les soon called for me to come up front.

"Here we go!" I thought.

"Tell Paul what you just told me," Les said to the little man at his desk. "He helped clean up the car."

"Hokay!" said the little man, smiling. "It is nice car. It run good. It start ever-day, 'RRR, pop,' start even in cold! I drive to work. Each day I drive now. No walk. Drive! Nice. My wife she like when I drive to church Sunday. She proud now. Already we drive maybe 100 miles! Only add one or two quarts oil!"

"He came back to tell us that!" said Les. "This is the first car he's ever owned, you know. He likes it."

"Well, when you wear it out you come back and we'll sell you another," I said, not knowing whether to laugh or cry or just thank the good Lord for how grateful I was. But I still worry about what I did to that '37 Ford 60.

Nick

Nick was a student of mine. I am not a teacher, but Nick needed a break each day from the tutoring he received from my wife, Jean, who is a qualified teacher. Each day Nick and I would work together on some project in my basement, like a foot stool, or a magnet, a metal lamp, anything that held Nick's interest for about a half hour each day.

At first Nick didn't show much interest, and I worked while he sometimes paid attention and sometimes didn't. What really got his attention on our first project was when I took out a can of varnish and asked him if he'd like to apply it to our work. It was good-bye brush and lots of runs, that first attempt, but pride was oozing from his every pore. After he left, and before the varnish dried, I sopped up the runs a bit and thought, "I'm getting through. He likes it."

By the time Nick left my attempt at tutoring, he could lay on a coat of paint or varnish like a pro and clean up the brush as well. Nick prided himself on keeping our work area cleaned up. He also made suggestions, and more than once told me I was making a mistake at one thing or another. He was thinking ahead.

"Measure twice, cut once," he'd say.

It had not been long after Nick started that we decided we would make two of each project, one for him and one for me. Nick had no desire to run the table saw, as he saw the potential danger therein, but he thrived on smaller power tools like sanders and drills, starting with the battery-powered tools.

Near his graduation from my wife and me, Nick had a show of all the things we had made together, plus some of his artwork from another teacher. Was I ever proud of Nick! I know his family was very proud of him, too.

It's been a year now since Nick has been on his own, making—and earning—his way in society. One thing I learned from Nick is that a loving family such as Nick's, and a little additional love thrown in by church and community, goes a long, long way in making a wonderful person.

When Nick first came to my wife for tutoring, he was eight; when he finished, he was eighteen. During those years I changed, a lot. I had retired early from a job in management where I preached perfection and quality for many years. Promotions in my department were based on performance, so I was always watchful, if not silently critical, of the progress of each employee under my jurisdiction.

Nick taught me a new way of measuring progress: it is not how great the speed to reach a goal, it's those little short spaced increments on the yardstick of life that measure advancement. It's not how much you achieve, it's the contentment you have in achieving it.

Measure twice, cut once.

"King George"

It was a dark and stormy night. The wind blew and the leaves flew with a fury not often encountered in late October. Then, after the storm, came the calm; all was quiet in the little old settlement of Unionville, Ohio.

Before the dawn came, however, the silence of the calm was shattered. Hours before I was ready to receive it, there came a loud announcement that morning was imminent. It came from a rooster perched just outside my bedroom window!

"Where did that come from!" groaned my wife, as though I could turn off the noise like I would an alarm clock.

"Something the wind blew in, I guess," might have been my response, with a few added adjectives.

By the time I got out of bed that morning, much earlier than I had planned, and way sooner than the alarm clock was set for, the crowing was coming from the front yard. And so I met "George" that morning, strutting about, pecking and scratching as happily as any rooster I had ever seen. He didn't pay me much attention, but I was curious about him.

There was something different about George, I noticed as I slowly approached him. He was sort of iridescent red and brown, not very large, and his comb was short. He edged his way over to the bushes surrounding my house, so I figured he would soon go home, wherever that was. That was all I saw of George till maybe five o'clock the next morning.

"That thing's gotta go," my wife and I said in unison. I got out of bed, got my flashlight, and found him perched about ten feet up in the blue spruce tree located right in front of our bedroom window. He was so happy to be announcing the arrival of another beautiful day that God made, I had to think maybe I should also be thankful, and happier about it than I was at that time in the morning.

George stayed. We called him George until one day some dear friends came to spend some time with us, and remembering that the woman of this couple had a brother named George, my wife, to my surprise, introduced our new family member as "King George." How fitting!

King George was as smart as any rooster I ever saw. One day a neighbor dog got loose and attacked George. Like a bullet George ran into the bushes heading north. The dog veered north to catch him upon exiting the bush. George exited south with a clear shot to the lower branches of the blue spruce, and up he went from branch to branch, like steps, to his hidden roost next to our bedroom window.

Snow fell. We had given George some scraps of food at first, but as the cold winter set in we began making sure he had feed and water. George didn't seem to be as obvious as the winter progressed, but he was not wild, almost friendly. We became used to his daily announcement of sunrise.

We fed him well all winter. Then one day early in the spring, my wife found that one of her friends had six chickens on her small farm and would be happy to add one more if King George needed a home.

By now we cared enough about King George that we wanted to find him a nice home.

So during the dark of night I gently picked George off his roost; no easy job climbing that tree! I brought him into our back entry, rocked him to sleep, and placed him on a step ladder. That seemed to suit King George just fine as he announced the arrival of the next day right on schedule . . . from within our house.

The day we gave King George away, I discovered he was tame, that is, he allowed himself to be handled. He was a fighting cock! His spurs had been removed, as had his comb and other vulnerable parts. I felt sorry for King George. I wondered if he had even fought, and if he would be a problem to the new owner to whom we were about to give him.

About a week later we heard the news. King George rose early every day, as usual. But what glorious days King George was spending! The six chickens were all hens. They had produced about one egg per day (for the flock). Then King George arrived. Now egg production was up to five and six per day, and all the hens were as happy as only King George could make them! He was now "King George of the Roost."

King George died—happy!—many years later. We missed him when he left.

Dream On!

Sometimes the good Lord needs to give you a nudge to arouse your talents; at least, that's what happened to me. I had not been working in an engineering department very long before I found myself as part of a team assigned to a problem that was causing major concerns for the company. If this problem product was not vastly improved, very soon, there was a strong likelihood the company would lose sales to our competitors. As part of this team we were working overtime every weekday, plus all day Saturdays.

I was a draftsman, and as such I could see that all of the changes being made had very little to do with correcting the major problems with the product. Although many minor changes might improve the product, there were major problems that had not been resolved.

One evening when I arrived home, exhausted, I took a short nap. When I awoke, I realized that in my dream I had redesigned a major portion of the product, or rather, the God-given gift of creativity had been awakened within me and I had been presented with a simple solution to a major problem.

The next morning I took a few minutes from my regular assignment, sketched my "gift," and presented it to my supervisor. At first he was polite and vaguely interested. Then he became more serious as he examined it. Then he picked it up and took it away. Later, he returned with the sketch and told me to roll up all the stuff I had been working on and go to work making my sketch an actual design.

A few days later it happened again, and in my dream was another new concept to correct many more of the product deficiencies. Shortly thereafter came a third dream, with more solutions. With that, my career as a draftsman ended, and career as a designer who dreamed a lot began.

I still create in my sleep; sometimes it's pictures (I think in pictures), sometimes it's music, sometimes it's poetry, sometimes it's wild stories. It always amazes me and makes me very mindful of, and thankful for, my real Creator.

My Last Cigarette

My last cigarette WAS my last cigarette. I had placed it between my lips and was about to light it up with my trusty Ronson lighter. I flicked the lighter; it fired-up first try.

"Don't light that cigarette!" a voice within me said. "Wait, smoke it later." So I put it back in the pack as I walked to my car after visiting the doctor's office.

At work, as a design engineer for Caterpillar, I was in my glory. My design had turned from concept to drawing; from drawing to blueprints; from blueprints to build date, to cutting iron, to prototype, to field testing, to full production of product, complete with serial numbers. I was riding high.

At home, my life was complete. My wife and I had bought, at an auction, a century-old home that really needed our tender loving care. We would raise our growing family there. Our little ones didn't care if we ever finished working on it, as the entire downstairs served as a race track for tricycles, wagons, and fire trucks. I had a lot to look forward to. Life was fun.

At work I began spending most of my time in the factory to follow the assembly and testing of the new product. The shop was noisy, so I had to raise my voice in order to be heard.

It was at this time that a friend of mine asked me to sing in his barbershop quartet. This friend had a wonderful lead tenor voice. He and I had sung duets at church, for which we had received many compliments. I had never been interested in singing barbershop, so I told my friend I would only sing in his quartet until he found someone to take the opening permanently. It was while singing with his quartet that I discovered there was something not right with my voice.

It wasn't long before I noticed that my voice seemed strained and raspy as I tried to speak up in the noisy factory. I noticed, too, that if I smoked a cigarette, something changed, the irritation, if it was an irritation, seemed to let up and I could talk louder, not necessarily easier. My wife noticed the change, too, so it was soon off to see our faithful family doctor with me.

Dr. Wallin looked at my voice box. It was tough to let him do that, as one gags with a dental mirror poked way down one's throat. But he saw enough wrong to send me to "Old" Doc Woodruff, an ear, nose, and throat specialist in nearby Joliet. Dr. Woodruff had a very fitting name; rough wood has a lot of splinters. But I learned to love that man; he challenged me! By the time Dr. Woodruff finished with me, he could take the dental mirror and poke it all around, bumping into that little hangy-down thing in my throat, and I could take it with total confidence he would not let go of it. He challenged me to cut down on smoking. I showed him! It was upon leaving his office that the voice shouted to me, "Don't smoke it."

When I was ready, Dr. Woodruff sent me to a well-known specialist in Chicago, Dr. Paul Hollinger. When he knew I could handle it, he operated. In the recovery room after the operation, I almost cried as one of the four of us he had operated on earlier in the day lit up a cigarette, and the doctor told him he might just as well. The prognosis for the others was not good either, but to me he spoke encouragingly. I needed that. Earlier that morning Jean had told me she had morning sickness. It would be our last child she was carrying.

The next two weeks I was silent. Told not to talk, I wrote notes. I had to laugh (silently of course) when I wrote my neighbor a note, handed it to him, and he wrote on the pad before handing it back. So I wrote on the pad, "I can hear!"

I smoked that last cigarette. I wanted to know if quitting was always going to be as hard as it had been the first two weeks. It would never get easier.

My problems were not over. It wasn't long before I was back in Chicago visiting Dr. Hollinger because something was wrong with my voice again, and I was no longer spending much time in the factory. I prayed the doctor could help me because between the time he had operated on my voice and this visit, less that a year later, two of my coworkers had died of throat cancer. I was scared.

Dr. Hollinger sent me directly from his office to Presbyterian-St. Luke's Hospital in Chicago. Here, that same day, after more exams and tests I began taking voice lessons! Me, who had sung all my life! Yes, I practiced breathing. I practiced a little ditty about "nay, nee, na, no, new." Every day I practiced. The objective was to lower the dominant pitch of my voice to avoid irritating the area of vocal cord which had been removed.

Some days my voice tires. Sometimes it falters when I sing, or try to speak loudly. Some days I have to go through the breathing exercises and sing the vowels. As I go through them, I think how happy I am that over forty years ago I smoked that last cigarette.

The Ronson Lighter

It was about a month after I quit smoking that my fellow workers in the engineering department began complimenting me on my self-discipline. One by one they had come to tell me that they had tried, without success, to quit. They wanted to know how I had done it.

One, Jim, told me he had quit smoking, at one time, for twelve years. Then he let down his guard and tried smoking one cigarette. He said that cigarette was awful, yet he lit another just to see if it would also be awful. He was hooked again, and couldn't shake it even for a day after that.

So I reached in the drawer of my drafting board and handed him my Ronson lighter.

"Here," I said, "you take this lighter and use it. And every time you light up take a look at the engraving on that lighter. It says, 'PTH.' Every time you light up just think, 'If PTH can do it, so can I.' I've just put a curse on that lighter as I handed it to you."

About a week later Jim told me he had not had a cigarette all day. "That damn lighter . . . it finally got to me, I can't smoke thinking you can quit and I can't. Here, take it back!"

I told him to keep it, I didn't want it back.

It wasn't long before Ron, another engineer, stopped by my board and showed me the Ronson lighter.

"Jim says you put a curse on this lighter. If I use it, I'll quit smoking. Mind if I use it?"

"No, I don't mind if you use it; I gave it to Jim and told him he could pass it on. I hope the curse gets to you, too."

It did. Ron quit smoking within another week. Within a month another engineer stopped by to show me that Ronson with PTH engraved on it.

"It's worth a try," he said. And he quit smoking.

About a year later, the Ronson was sitting on my drafting board with a note under it saying the curse had been lost and the writer of the note was sorry it hadn't worked for him as it had for me. But, he said, he couldn't continue using it because it made him feel guilty.

I don't remember what happened to that lighter, but for years three engineers felt compelled to tell me they were still smoke-free.

"Watch out for that twelfth year," I'd respond to Jim, and for Ron I'd say, "Watch out for each day. Stay on guard!"

I still do that. Each day. It works for me.

Accosted!

"Aren't you afraid you'll be accosted?" my mother-in-law asked, when my wife told her she was playing piano for a jazz band. For a long time we laughed about that . . . until the night my wife was playing for the jazz band and I was accosted as I sat in the audience. It happened like this:

I was sitting with my two friends, minding my own business, when a beautiful young woman came to our table and sat in the empty chair between Tony and me and asked me to explain to her what ragtime music is. My, she was pleasant to look at. She was stylishly dressed, wore high heels, had a lovely figure and had a disposition suitable to be a school teacher. . . . Sunday school teacher, we thought.

I was highly complimented to think she would ask me about ragtime and began telling her all the nuances of the music as she gazed smilingly into my eyes and placed her hand on the back of my chair. About this time, as I began to slur my words and lose my train of thought, Tony began to show great interest in the conversation. This allowed Ted, my other friend, to lean over the table to get a closer look at this doll and also listen in, in case I lost my place or said the wrong things to this attractive lady.

This was my clue to involve my friends in the conversation as I was becoming somewhat self-conscious—and besides, my wife can play the piano quite well without looking at the keys. I assumed she had not noticed but later discovered she had witnessed the entire scene that had and was about to take place. So did the rest of the band.

Because Teddy entered the conversation, our guest switched her attention to him, so much so, I'm afraid, that she switched from her chair to sitting on Ted's knee. Teddy's eyes rolled back as though to say, "What do I do with her now?" But really he was trying not to scream in pain as she had sat on his bad knee. Ted sort of put his arms around her to shift her around a bit and she in turn put her arms around the back of his chair.

Tony laughed. I sighed. Tony said something to Ted that made Ted laugh, and laughing made his knee hurt even more. But it didn't matter, the woman had noticed Tony's hair.

"What beautiful hair!" she exclaimed, as she transferred from Ted's bad knee to Tony's full lap and began running both hands through his silvery grey shoulder-length distinguished-looking hair. All Tony could say was, "Don't do that," like he was going to pass out if she continued.

Enter now another person. A man. Her date. She told him to go away; she was having a good time with these nice men. He left.

So what do we do now, we guys asked each other with our eyes, not speaking a word. But she caught on, laughed, and said she just wanted to get rid of that guy, as he was a terrible bore. As the guy stomped out she removed herself from Tony's lap and sat properly in the chair next to me again. Now she acted more like a Sunday school teacher.

It was time for a break for the band so my wife joined us. She had a strange look on her face that said, "What's going on here?" The woman politely said goodbye to all of us and departed to where she had come from, I presume.

Tony, Ted, and I have never lived this event down. Only my wife witnessed the event; Tony and Ted were batching it that night, but between my wife, plus all the members of the band, there were no secrets kept, and shortly all three wives knew every glorious detail about the night all three of us were accosted.

My wife keeps telling me she thinks the woman had been over-served adult beverages, but the three of us who were accosted like to think this lady just had good taste in men, so she chose us!

Ghosts

Autumn is my favorite season of the year. I like it for all the same reasons as everyone else . . . the colors, the cooling, the romance, the memories. And Halloween, with ghost stories. Of course, most people don't believe in ghosts, so this story will sound made up, but for those of us who were there, this is not fantasy.

On a visit to my wife's brother Bill in Boggstown, Indiana, Jean and I were very tired after driving all day and playing our music late into the night. It was good to get some sleep. We slept upstairs, over the restaurant where we played. Very convenient. We went right to sleep. Later I arose to use the bathroom. On the way, I got a chill . . . my hair rose on end . . . I felt the presence of something.

"Spooky place," I thought. In the bathroom I heard noises coming from the restaurant bathroom directly below.

"Someone is still here besides me, my wife, and Bill," I reasoned. My brother-in-law Bill was the executive chef and lived alone in the apartment above the restaurant. I'd ask him about it in the morning. I sleepily returned to bed. But Jean was sitting up in bed and whispered, "Did you hear that noise?"

"Yes," I said. "I think Carlos is down there." Carlos owned the place.

"It sounded like an angry mob," said my wife.

"What are you talking about?" I asked.

"I heard noises like a horse-drawn wagon . . . and chairs rattling . . . and voices. I couldn't make out what they were talking about and I couldn't see them from the window. What's going on?"

I responded with, "Well I wasn't alone when I went to the bathroom either; we'll ask Bill about it tomorrow." So we slept . . . close together, I might add.

Next morning I got up before anyone else, as usual, went to the kitchen and turned on the light. I sat there reading until Bill got up, entered the kitchen, and said, "I see you've figured out the light switches already."

"Is there something wrong with them?" I asked.

"Yeah, you have to walk all the way through the room in the dark to find the switch on the far side, or didn't you notice?" said Bill.

"I just used this switch," I said, pointing to the one right next to me.

"It doesn't work," said Bill. "Even the electrician can't make it work." So I got up and flicked the switch off and on a couple of times to prove my point. Bill looked amazed as he tried it, too. It didn't work for him.

"You have to hold your mouth just right," I joked as I did it again and it worked. "By the way, Bill, did someone stay over, or come back, after we closed last night?"

"No," replied Bill. "Like that light switch, funny things just happen out here in the country; you'll get used to it."

Before we opened for the evening, my wife and I were practicing in the restaurant when the waitresses arrived to set up the tables. As they sat folding napkins, one of them asked us if the ghost had welcomed us yet.

"Oh, don't tell them that stuff," said another waitress. "There aren't any ghosts around here."

At that moment the silverware from a table about ten feet from where they were sitting fell to the floor. The table seated eight . . . all the silverware fell!

"Well," said the second waitress, "you didn't have to mention it their first day!"

That night after we closed, the waitresses, the kitchen help, the owner and entertainers were sitting around a table in the lobby just relaxing and rehashing the events of the evening, when the outer entry door opened. I was closest to the entry door and waited for the inner door to open, but it didn't. I suspected someone had opened and closed the outer door without entering. Then the inner door opened and closed, but no one entered. The outer door opened and closed again, so I ran out through the inner door and outer door to see who it was that kept opening doors but not entering. No one was there. I ran around the entire building. No one. As I entered to join the others I just said, "Nobody was there." Nobody?

One of the other entertainers was from Illinois. After we performed, he enjoyed a considerable amount of wine before retiring. Next morning when he got up, he sat there drinking coffee and asked Chef, "Who was that playing the piano about three o'clock this morning?" So the chef confirmed to us that there was a ghost, or two, or three hanging around, and if we just ignored them most of the time they were no problem.

With that our friend from Illinois got up from the table, packed his car, and went back home, never to return.

The next night I heard Chef yell out in the middle of the night "Bug off! Dammit!" Then all was quiet. Next morning I asked him who he was yelling at. Did he have company?

"No, a ghost kept kicking my foot 'til I yelled at her to bug off. I must have done something she didn't like," replied Chef.

"How do you know it's a she?" I asked.

"Because sometimes she cooks things at night and makes me get up and check out all the burners and ovens in the middle of the night. She cooks things I don't have on the menu; they smell good. Other times she just kicks me, not hard, just enough to wake me up."

I was beginning to wonder about Chef. When my wife got up, we went to the kitchen for orange juice, and one of the help arrived. We were teasing Chef about his night visitor when the employee said she hadn't been bothered by the ghost for a long, long time. With that, the clock on the wall behind us fell with a crash onto a stack of dishes.

"Well, up until now," she added as she went off to work.

The owner's wife told us she saw a man in a plaid shirt and overalls standing in the kitchen one day. She approached him and asked if she could help him, but he vanished.

"He could have used a shave," she said.

One night as we drove off with Chef, the lights went on in the upstairs bathroom as we were backing out of his garage.

"Not again," said Chef as he left my wife and me saying he wanted those lights off. We were puzzled. We hadn't noticed they were on; maybe we left them on, not Chef. He hardly reached the back door when the lights went off, but he entered not knowing that. Soon he returned and said, "Watch this . . . watch the bathroom."

As he started the car the lights in the bathroom went on.

"She's mad at me again," said Chef as we drove off.

Next morning we were to leave by seven to make it back to Cleveland for an afternoon job. At five-thirty that morning, the alarm and radio in the living room blasted out as loud as possible.

"Chef must want to feed us breakfast before we go," I said to my wife.

"I'd rather sleep," said she.

I opened the door to tell Chef we were awake when here he came, running from his bedroom with a tired look on his face.

"Did you set the alarm for this early?" he asked.

"No, did you?" I replied. So we both stood and laughed. What else could we do?

For three years we played four days a month at that restaurant and stayed upstairs. If you ask us if we believe in ghosts we'll tell you yes, and we'd bet you would, too, if you ever stayed there.

Going Home

I don't consider myself to be a violent person. When I was in second grade and Fred Schmoeger was in fifth grade, but small for his age, we had a fight over a teeter-totter during recess. Miss Moran, the school principal, caught us. Miss Moran could strike fear in the devil himself when her laws were broken, and Fred and I had broken one of her laws. I don't believe Fred, or I, ever fought anyone ever again.

But I came close, very close, one night in the airport of São Paulo, Brazil. This little man from Tourismo (that's the name of the travel agency from whom our plane tickets had been purchased) had decided to sell our tickets to someone else.

Do you remember, as a child, being away from home for a few days and rediscovering all the things about home that you had missed? Do you remember returning home, or to your grandparents' home, to your hometown after being away for a long, long time and finding things the same, but finding you had changed by growing larger or more mature? In your memories, streets were wider, houses larger, and Mom and Dad younger. Home is a place of those types of memories.

Now imagine that you left the USA with your family and knew when you left it would be a year before you would return. The idea doesn't seem like much of a big deal to those who have never done it, but there is something different about being away from home with your family than being away on your own.

The first thing one learns while entering a foreign country is that the customs officers do not speak English, don't care if you speak English, and are not going to learn English to speak to you! If you don't understand what they say, they repeat it, louder, like it's your ears that are the problem. If you try to explain the importance of your mission or the importance of handling your packet of x-rays required by their government for you to become a resident in their country, they give you a blank stare with a snarling smile and simply toss your x-rays into a waste basket and move on to their next point of interrogation.

By the eighth month in Brazil, we felt it was important to procure our tickets, or at least make our reservations to return to the USA for our month of home leave. Reservations were made; no tickets appeared. Two months before take-off, reservations were confirmed, no tickets yet, but assurances that everything in the system was functioning properly.

Two weeks before take-off, the same story and a reminder to be sure to have your passports with you, and up-to-date, and be sure to have your foreign money exchanged for US dollars, $1,000 max.

Two days before take-off Tourismo announced they would have a representative meet us at the airport to be sure we are checked through properly and have no difficulty; a nice gesture of appreciation, we thought.

We were met at the airport, by this little man with a smile and friendly handshake. I would soon threaten to beat him to a bloody pulp. He asked us for our passports as we approached the ticket counter and then he handed them to the ticket agent.

"Where are our tickets?" I asked.

"He already has them," responded the little devil I was dealing with.

Our passports were then handed to someone who went into the room behind the ticket counter; we were told to wait for them to be "processed."

Now as fate would have it, a Brazilian friend and coworker had come to the airport to see us off. Well, I thought it was fate but it may have been this fine fellow had a suspicious mind and had come to see that we were handled correctly by the ticket agent.

As we talked, and waited, I was nervous about being separated from our passports, something you fear when in a foreign country.

As time passed, my Brazilian friend excused himself and went to speak to the ticket agent, then to the travel agent. I could tell he was pushing for answers and was being shrugged off, as those with authority learn to do when being the slightest bit pressured. Soon he darted into the room behind the ticket agent. When he returned, he told me I had better talk to the ticket agent, as our plane was loaded for departure. The ticket agent was trying to avoid us at this point.

"Why aren't we being called to board?" I demanded of the agent.

"There must be a problem. I will go check," he responded and took off. My Brazilian friend went with him whether the agent liked it or not.

When the agent returned he announced quite casually, "There has been a small problem. We have you now scheduled for the next flight to Rio where we will take you to a fine hotel, at our expense, and you will fly to the USA tomorrow night."

As I was catching my breath, he continued, "It was because the flight was over-booked and you made your reservations too late that you were bumped off the flight to the USA."

I had caught my breath . . . and him, by the front of his shirt, coat, and tie, and had lifted him off the ground about six inches as I pulled him face-to-face. I stomped my foot so hard on the mosaic tile floor the shot rang out and silence fell throughout the lobby as I issued a tirade of statements which included things like: "We will fly to the USA tonight, not tomorrow. We will not fly to Rio at your expense; we will spend that time arranging for the cancellation of your account with my company . . . starting with the President of the company back in the USA. I'll be working from that end on the problem, not this end on the problem." I then shook him a little bit and set him down preparing to punch if need be.

But this little man had changed. He was very cooperative. He ran and got our passports, he arranged for us to meet our flight to the USA at Rio and our flight would be waiting if we were late.

We arrived in Rio, our baggage already waiting . . . our four bags in the middle of the airport, alone! We were whisked through customs, quite roughly for the women, easily for the men; we were driven to the plane at the end of the runway, ready for take-off, encouraged to hurry up the loading ramp, and off we went to the USA.

You can't imagine the USA after you have lived in a foreign country! The customs officials were pleasant, not just to Americans. The air was clean and fresh, the sky blue, the sun bright, the trees green, the roads paved and clean, drivers considerate and driving safely, fast food places where you could eat the food . . . home.

My Brazilian friend learned that the next day the government was going to add a tax on everyone leaving Brazil. The tax would be $1,000, returnable one year later. Of course, one year later the currency would only be worth half, or less than half, due to inflation. Our travel agent had tried to save someone else $4,000 by using our four tickets. I hope he put them up in a fine hotel in Rio, but I don't worry much about it.

Dream Cars

Model A I already own the best car ever made regardless of price. It's a 1931 Ford, Model A.

After producing millions and millions of Model Ts throughout the teens and twenties of the twentieth century, Henry Ford knew what he wanted when he produced the Model A in the late twenties and early thirties.

When I was two years old my dad drove home in a brand-new 1929 Ford. That's the car I learned to drive and respect.

I bought my first Model A Ford right after WWII for $125. It had been driven 180,000 miles before I bought it. I drove it 60,000 more miles and sold it for $115. Total cost of operation per mile was under 2¢. That was one fun car. One night twelve of us crammed into it, and there were only three of us in the front seat.

Another 1929 I owned later was more of a challenge. I owned this Phaeton (four-door convertible) over a year before I could get it to drive all the way around the block. This was in Brazil, where I had to make my own parts, including a wheel bearing.

My favorite Model A is in full service today. Ready to go, licensed to drive, and I drive it all year. I've owned this one since 1963. All four of my children learned to drive in this car.

I would not propose manufacturing the Model A again. But I would propose that every prospective automotive engineer be required to take one apart and put it together. Each part is a lesson in function and simplicity.

Stanley Steamer   I was visiting my parents on the farm where my grandparents had lived all their lives, when a man dressed in white, with goggles on his forehead, knocked on the door. He looked like a WWI flying ace! But it was his 1914 Stanley Steamer, not a plane, that had broken down on the road in front of the farm.

Here he was, with his wife, forty miles from Dayton, with a flat tire and no spare. To make it worse, the tube had torn the valve stem out, ruining it. The man didn't know what to do, nor whom to call as he was from New Jersey and was just visiting Dayton to show his Steamer at an auto show.

"We can probably find a tube in the barn," I told the man.

"A thirty-two-inch tube?" the man asked. "One that would hold air?"

"Let's look," I said.

Well, we came up with a twenty-one-inch Firestone

inner tube that was purchased at the Chicago World's Fair of 1933–34. "Gum dipped" it said on the side. We used binder twine to stretch it out inside the large thirty-two-inch tire. It worked.

Then came the thrill of watching the Stanley Steamer come to life. One starts a Stanley with a match! Slowly it begins to percolate. Not much later, it silently moves, save for a low hissing noise, and cruises off. What a car! We may live to see its revival someday.

My Barn

My most prized possession is a barn. Actually, my most prized possession is shared with my wife, and that would be our marriage license, which she paid for over fifty years ago. But the story of the marriage license is short; I had forgotten to bring money the day we went for our license. So my most prized possession, as an object, is a barn.

As we were searching for a place to live, when we arrived in Ohio, our realtor, who was spending her days showing us property and her nights searching for property to show us, drove past this house as we were going to lunch at the Old Tavern in Unionville.

"There's a nice house for sale," my wife announced, and sure enough, there was a man pounding a "for sale" sign into the frozen ground. My eye caught the barn.

"There's a . . . barn, too!" I added with hesitation, trying to show enthusiasm. I had not really seen the house at all, just the sorry-looking barn. I wanted a barn. I needed a barn.

The next day I dutifully toured through the house with my wife and agreed with all the comments she made about things she liked, the things she would change, about how nice it would be for the two of us to have seven bedrooms available for visiting grandchildren . . . should we ever have any grandchildren.

When it came time to tour the barn, which was what I wanted to see first but was polite and saved for last, I was a little disappointed. First of all, the realtor informed me she had learned from the appraisal of the property that the barn had been valued at zero dollars. That was very revealing. It would cost money to fix the barn, or it would cost money to tear it down, so how could a building be worth zero dollars when in fact it was a liability? My interpretation of the appraisal was to deduct from the asking price some amount before making an offer. It worked. But what the sellers didn't know was they could have raised the price and my wife would have agreed because she wanted the house so much. And I wanted the barn.

The house has been a jewel. It was built one year after the barn. The barn was built in 1837. The only things wrong with

the barn were one corner post had rotted out and that corner was 18 inches lower than the other corners; nearly every window was broken, or the frames were missing altogether; the roof leaked; the floor fell through while I was standing on it; its lower level was full of sand that had flooded in from rainwater runoff which ran through the barn's upper ground-level side; the siding was loose, falling off, rotted off at the bottoms; there were birds, bees, wasps, and a spot on the wooden floor where there was telltale evidence that someone had built a bonfire that, luckily, went out before burning the entire structure.

It only took me about twenty years to fix my barn. My father used to tell me people would be sorry if they neglected their barns, that they were irreplaceable, and should be cared for. I believe he was right. Barns are great to have.

Now here is what is so amazing about barns. Barns produce goods! Barns always need cleaning out. Barns are where you find stuff you're looking for. Barns are where you put stuff you know you'll be looking for someday. Barns provide filler for yard sales. Barns invite friends. Children return home with loads and loads of stuff to store and forget about. And because this barn is mine (my wife very seldom enters the barn) people who need to ask, "Do you know where I can find a . . . ?" (fill in the blank) can come to me, and chances are I will have at least one, in my beautiful barn.

Faith

Sitting in church one Sunday, my wife of forty-six years nudged me and pointed to her engagement ring. The diamond was missing! We searched the pew around us and studied the floor. After the service, we examined her coat pockets, gloves, purse, car, walkway, entry, bedroom, bed, vacuum bag before and after vacuuming the entire house. What next, the plumbing? The yard?

"No, we'll wait and keep the faith. We'll find it," she said.

All week we kept our eyes open extra wide, sort of like we were playing hide-the-thimble; never giving up, but the chance of finding it faded, and the adjustment of accepting that it was lost became stronger.

The loss of the diamond did not alter our feelings toward each other. If the diamond was a symbol of loving forever, it was apparent that it had served its purpose well, and our love would continue long after the symbolism was gone.

Then came Saturday night. We had company for dinner and they had to leave early. As they left, they asked us if we were going to go back to the restaurant where we had listened to a jazz band the Saturday before. It seemed like a good idea and we all discussed the merits of taking a flashlight, just to look around for the diamond.

As we entered the room of the restaurant where we had been the week before, the first beam of light, from way across the room, hit the diamond. It was safely tucked in a corner, waiting for the faithful.

On the way home, I said to my wife, "We never reported the lost diamond to our insurance company!"

"There wasn't any need to," she said. "I knew we'd find it."

This story was published in Lake County Council on Aging newspaper, *The Bridge*.

ACKNOWLEDGMENTS

THANK YOU TO those who have been so generous in sharing their memories and photos for this book:

Our mother, Agnes Huling, for keeping a scrapbook, which she passed on to me. It contained stories and other memorabilia regarding her contribution to the war effort while commuting and working at GROP (Green River Ordnance Plant) near Dixon, Illinois.

Jean Hahne Huling for making brother Paul's collection of stories available to me.

James M. Huling for his honest story about work. "Hard work ain't easy." His avocation is music. During his high school years he performed in three bands: The Rising Tides, Cochise, and Buckacre. He has cut his first CD, entitled "Old Friends." It's available at cdbaby.com

PHOTO CREDITS

INDEX

Photographs indicated in *bold italic*

USS General Brooke, 37
Utah Beach, France, 34
Utica Four Corners, IL, 129
V-1 flying bomb, 26
V-E Day, 37, 62
V-J Day, 37
WACs, 48
Wacker, John, 49, 105
Wakefield, Warren, 37-38, 41-47, 56; *32*, *35*
Wall Street, 24
Wallin, Doctor, 168
War Department, 11
Warren, Harlan, 113

Washington D.C., 56, 108
Washington, PA, 103
Wellesley, MA, 141
White Fence Farm, 115
Whitefish Bay, 112
Wilmot, Harry J., 119-120
Witte, E. J. , 62
Woodruff, Doctor, 168
Wylepski, Emil, 116
Yelich, Teddy, 15
Younger, Marilyn, 125, 127
Younger, Ray, 125
Zera, Mr., 122
Ziegenburg, Germany, 53